CAREERS WITH DOGS

By Audrey Pavia

BARRON'S

All inquiries should be addressed to:
Barron's Educational Series, Inc.
250 Wireless Boulevard
Hauppauge, New York 11788
http://www.barronseduc.com

International Standard Book No. 0-7641-0503-5

Library of Congress Catalog Card No. 98-13029

᾿

Library of Congress Cataloging-in-Publication Data

Pavia, Audrey.
    Careers with dogs / by Audrey Pavia.
        p.   cm.
    Includes bibliographical references and index.
    ISBN 0-7641-0503-5
    1. Dog industry—Vocational guidance.   I. Title.
SF426.55.P38   1998   98-13029
636.7'0023'73—dc21   CIP

Printed in the United States of America

9   8   7   6   5   4   3   2   1

DEDICATION

To my mentor Marion Lane, who not only gave me my first break in the dog world but also her enduring friendship.

ACKNOWLEDGMENTS

I would like to thank the following people and organizations for their help with this book:

Barron's editors Grace Freedson and Anna E. Damaskos; attorney Roberta Kraus; Macintosh whiz Doug Kraus; my friend and colleague Betsy Sikora Siino; my sister and ace veterinary technician Heidi Pavia D'Anna; veterinarian and friend Janice M. Posnikoff, D.V.M.; my friend, colleague, and obedience instructor Liz Palika; my ever-supportive husband Randy Mastronicola; Marti Kincaid of the National Association of Dog Obedience Instructors; Jacque Schultz of the American Society for the Prevention of Cruelty to Animals; petsitter Richard A. Nelhs; the editors at *Dog Fancy* magazine; the North American Veterinary Technician Association; the American Boarding Kennels Association; the Association of Pet Dog Trainers; and the National Animal Control Association.

Audrey Pavia
Laguna Hills, California

TABLE OF CONTENTS

One—A Close Partnership   1
In the Beginning   1
Dog's Work   3
Turning the Tide   4
How It All Turned Out   6

Two—Working With Dogs   8
Do You Have What It Takes?   8
The Good and the Bad   11

Three—Marketing Yourself   15
Choosing the Right Job   15
Getting Prejob Experience   18
Getting Your Foot in the Door   20
That Important Paperwork   24
The Interview   26

Four—Health Care Professions   28
Veterinarian   29
Veterinary Technician   36
Veterinary Assistant   41

Five—Jobs in General Dog Care   45
Boarding Kennel Operator   46
Kennel Aide   50
Petsitter   53

Six—Humane Work   59
Animal Welfare Advocate   60
Animal Control Officer   65

Seven—Hands-On Work   **70**
Dog Trainer   71
Obedience Instructor   75
Groomer   80
Professional Handler   85

Eight—Corporate Professions   **91**
Marketing Specialist   92
Editor   95
Attorney   100

Nine—Creative Positions   **105**
Commercial Artist   106
Commercial Photographer   111
Freelance Writer   116

Appendix   **122**

Index   **136**

A CLOSE PARTNERSHIP

IN THE BEGINNING

 Imagine a dark, cold night nearly 15,000 years ago. Men, women, and children in tattered furs cluster around a large fire, each clutching meat-covered bones in their hands. As they dine voraciously on what's left of the day's hunt, a pair of yellow eyes glows in the shadows beyond them.

One of the humans glances up and, from the corner of her eye, sees the animal. She recognizes a primitive wolf, one of the predators that shares the land her clan calls home. Impulsively, she pulls a scrap of meat from the bone and tosses it to the animal. Snatching the morsel, the wolf carries it but a few feet away. As the wolf swallows the gift, the two creatures make eye contact. Somewhere in that moment, the beginnings of the canine/human bond is formed.

Many scientists believe that scenarios such as this one, repeated over and over again in the Pleistocene era, eventually led to the domestication of the dog some 10,000 years ago. While it's not clear exactly why primitive humans accepted the wolf into their culture, there is speculation that the animal served both a practical and spiritual purpose in early human life. Those special wolves—individuals drawn to the fires of primitive humans and their pups raised by human hand—eventually became domesticated canids that learned to accept their human food givers as members of their own pack.

Protecting their human family members as they would their own, these early domesticated dogs began to serve as sentries, detecting the sound of approaching enemies and warning their people long before the humans would have discovered it for themselves. It is possible these dogs even hunted side by side with their two-legged companions, helping to bring home precious sources of protein and fat in which they would also partake. Over time, these same primitive dogs would develop into livestock guardians, protecting domesticated hooved animals as if they were a part of their own pack.

These dogs gave their masters much of what our own dogs of today provide to us: affection, devotion, and a link to the nonhuman animal world. It is not hard to see why primitive humans were so drawn to these amazing creatures, keeping them close at hand.

DOG'S WORK

 While early humans may have been in awe of the dog in large part because of its endearing qualities, much of their attraction was based on the fact that the dog could help them survive. Life was hard in ancient times, and people soon discovered that canine devotion could be channeled into means that would help ensure human survival. From the time of primitive man to the dawn of the great civilizations, dogs were put to heavy work. They hunted for their master's food, guarded his home, and toiled as beasts of burden. They even served as a source of food when nothing else was available.

However, time was on the dog's side. As human culture began to blossom and the great Egyptian civilization prevailed, the dog's position in the human world started to evolve. While the dogs of ancient Egypt worked for a living by hunting for their masters, they also became highly valued as companions by Egyptian citizens of every status. The ancient Greeks and Romans, who lived at the time, also treasured their dogs not merely as hunters but as pets as well.

Although it was becoming more highly regarded, the dog of the great civilizations was not the finely crafted creature that it is now. Dogs of the time bred indiscriminately among themselves, since the ancients knew little about selective breeding. The idea of deliberately breeding dogs for certain traits did not take hold until the Renaissance, when hunting became a diversion of the elite. Well-bred hunting dogs accompanied their wealthy masters in the field as they brought down game merely for the sport of it. In the meantime, privileged ladies became fond of tiny dogs they could keep on their laps, and heavy breeds were used for guarding feudal castles. Not only the rich owned dogs in Medieval times: jobs like herding, pulling carts, and turning kitchen turnspits were performed by the dogs of the working class.

Meanwhile, in other areas of human culture, dogs were in charge of more gruesome duties. Attack dogs were an integral part of the Spanish conquest of the New World, their trainability and dedication exploited to help destroy the culture of the natives who lived on non-European shores. These dogs served as enforcers of cruel and unfair laws and were the weapon of choice against the dominated peoples.

Before the Spaniards made their way westward to perform these duties, native peoples in both North and South America lived closely with dogs of their own. Curly tailed, thick-coated Nordic dogs pulled the sleds of the northern-most peoples, and medium-sized, sharp-muzzled canines dragged the travois of the Plains. Closer to the equator, hairless dogs brought warmth to the people who owned them and even became objects of worship.

Although the dog was slowly becoming closer to the human heart, it wasn't until the Industrial Revolution that the dog's role in human society began to change drastically from worker to pet. Purebred dogs became all the rage in England, and dog shows literally became the sport of queens. This new attitude toward the dog—whose traditional role of toiler was rapidly being replaced by machines—garnered a strong foothold.

Now, more than 100 years later, the dog's position in human society as a devoted companion is firmly secured. No further justification of the dog's presence in our world is needed. He is here because we want him here. He is here because he has become our closest friend.

TURNING THE TIDE

 Dogs have spent nearly all of the past 10,000 years working for humankind. With the exception of the last two centuries, the dog existed primarily to help us get along in our daily lives. But in our mechanized world of today, there is little need for a dog to work the turnspit or pull a cart filled with goods for market. Yet we continue to be drawn to the dog with more passion than ever. Why is this?

We have gained much with our advancements in technology, but we have lost something very important at the same time. We no longer care much about the plants that grow in the forest or the proximity of a clear running river. The ways of wild animals are not important to us anymore. Water flows to our homes from faucets, and everything we eat is the product of a trip to the grocery store. We have become far removed from nature as a result of our modern life. In fact, most of us feel more in tune with our computers than with the natural world around us.

Here is where the dog comes in. In our present-day world, *canis familiaris* serves a vital role. The dog provides us with a link to our once-wild selves, a real attachment to the planet Earth we call our home, a connection we desperately need. Without it, we lose our perspective in the world and fail to understand who we really are.

This is why many dogs today are viewed by those who love them as members of the family, creatures whose purpose is not to help us survive physically, as in the past, but spiritually and psychologically in today's world. While there are still dogs who work for a living—police dogs, assistance dogs, and military dogs are just a few—primarily, it is we humans who are now working *for the dog*.

Looking at the dog's history of service to mankind, it is nothing short of ironic to see how the tables have turned. Yet, that is exactly what has happened. Because we think of dogs as members of our society, they are granted great privileges. Well-cared-for dogs are groomed regularly. They eat only the best-quality dog food and wear only the finest collars. They are seen by a veterinarian regularly so their health can be maintained, and they are boarded at special facilities when their families are away. Today's dogs are even specially trained to behave as one should in human society. And why not? They are an important, if not integral, part of our world.

Dogs today are written about, litigated over, painted, and photographed. They are memorialized, eulogized, and celebrated.

There is no end to the ways dogs have been incorporated into the human family, and no end to the way they will continue to be.

It is because of all this that you are here, reading this book. Where it once took considerable dog power to service mankind, it now takes considerable manpower to serve the dog. With each aspect of the dog's connection to humanity comes a job, a task that needs doing. And for those of us who love dogs, this is a labor of love.

HOW IT ALL TURNED OUT

 The result of all this passion for dogs is the pet industry, a multibillion dollar trade dedicated to pampering our pets. A myriad of businesses throughout North America exist solely to provide products and services to dog owners, and scores of jobs in these fields are ready to be had.

There are a lot of dog owners out there. In 1996, more than 37 million American households owned dogs. This was up slightly from the year before, which was up slightly from the year before that. Dog ownership continues to grow in North America, and products and services to meet the needs of canines and their families are in high demand.

This is where you come in. You can choose to work in the veterinary health care profession, treating sick and injured dogs who need your help every day. Or, you can start your own pet supply store, selling dog food and accessories to the people in your community. You can even go to work as an animal control officer, ensuring that dogs in your jurisdiction are treated fairly and humanely.

Because so much of the pet industry is made up of corporate structure, desk jobs relating to dogs abound. All that dog food and all those toys need to be marketed to the dog-owning public, and if you are a salesperson at heart, this might be the position for you.

Dog-related information is also a business within the pet industry, and editors who know about both dogs and publishing are needed in this field.

All in all, the business of dogs is booming, and this is good news for those dedicated animal lovers who want a profession in one of the many canine-related fields. For those of us who choose a career with dogs, the future looks more than promising.

WORKING WITH DOGS

DO YOU HAVE WHAT IT TAKES?

 If you are reading this book, you undoubtedly have a great passion for all things canine. When you see a dog and its owner walking down the street, you can't help but stop and turn your head to get a good look—at the pooch, of course. While flipping through the channels on your television set, you stop right away if a dog appears on the screen. And if you are away from your own dog for too long, you start to feel as if you are undergoing symptoms of withdrawal.

It is no wonder then that you are considering a career working with dogs. And well you should. An intense interest in and great love of dogs are mandatory if you plan to spend the rest of your working life thinking, breathing, and living the subject of man's best friend.

EMPATHY

Depending on which type of canine career you intend to pursue, there are other qualities besides a love of dogs that you must also possess. If the job you are considering means working hands-on with dogs on a daily basis, you must have a great deal of empathy and patience for animals. Whether you are working as a trainer, groomer, veterinarian, or kennel aide, you will find yourself in situations where the animal you are trying to help is not happy about what you are doing. Are you the type of person who can understand the dog's mental state, and feel compassion and sympathy toward the animal? Or do you imagine you will feel extremely irritated by a dog that tries to struggle or resist, or becomes aggressive toward you?

If you see yourself as being patient and understanding in even the most difficult dog-related situations, you are a good candidate for a hands-on career with dogs. If you love dogs but think you may be short on patience under stressful circumstances, consider one of the many careers that deal with dogs as a subject rather than on an individual basis. Your days will still be consumed with dogs, but you won't have to worry about a daily struggle with your emotions.

PEOPLE SKILLS

Many people gravitate toward working with animals because they do not enjoy working with people. Animals can be challenging to deal with at times, but a problem dog is often a lot easier to handle than a problem human. Many animal lovers prefer the company of animals to other humans and hope that they will avoid dealing with people if they pursue a career with dogs.

Unfortunately, this couldn't be farther from the truth. There is not one dog-related profession that doesn't call for skills dealing with humans. Dogs are domesticated animals and, by definition, are closely attached to the human race. If you are considering a career in canine health care, keep in mind that you will be interacting daily with pet owners and other health care professionals. If you want to be a dog trainer or obedience instructor, you will find yourself trying to communicate as much with humans as with dogs. Even artists who specialize in painting dogs have considerable contact with humans, since the work they are creating is for the dog's owner, not the dog.

Given all this, it's important to examine your inner self to determine whether or not you like people enough to work with dogs. If you are determined to find a job where you have minimal contact with humans, a career in the dog-related professions is not a good choice for you.

LOVE OF ALL ANIMALS

There are some people who profess to love dogs but have little use for other animals. If you are one of these individuals, there will be limited canine-career choices for you.

A great number of hands-on dog-related careers require interaction with other animals, particularly cats. Veterinarians, veterinary technicians, veterinary assistants, kennel aides, boarding kennel operators, petsitters, groomers, and a multitude of other dog-related professions include dealing with cats on a regular basis. Notable exceptions to this are professional handlers, trainers, and obedience instructors. If you have a real aversion to working with cats, you will be limited to one of these professions. (Keep in mind that many corporate and creative positions also involve cats and other pets.)

GOOD HEALTH

You don't have to be a weight lifter to work hands-on with dogs, but a strong upper body and healthy back can be a great help. Veterinarians, veterinary technicians, veterinary assistants, groomers, trainers, and even petsitters and kennel aides often find themselves in situations where they have to lift a heavy dog.

Allergies can also be a health concern. If you are determined to work with dogs but have allergies to them, you should see your doctor about the possibility of allergy shots.

Another option if you are an allergy sufferer is to consider a position that won't require you to be around pets on a constant basis. Groomers and those in the health care professions are particularly prone to allergic situations. (Even if you are not allergic to dogs, keep in mind that an allergy to cats can cause you problems in certain dog-related careers.)

THE GOOD AND THE BAD

Working with dogs has its pluses and minuses. No job is perfect, but it's important to examine both the problems and the benefits associated with a canine career so you can make an educated decision about whether or not this is the right field for you.

DISADVANTAGES

Money: Like many intensely rewarding professions, working with dogs does not normally reap great financial rewards. With few exceptions, people who maintain careers with dogs have resigned themselves to making a small to moderate living. Even veterinarians, who are the top of the canine-career pay scale, don't usually get rich while attending to the health needs of their clients.

There are exceptions to this general rule, however few. There are some high-profile dog trainers with famous Hollywood clients who charge significant fees to work with the dogs of the wealthy.

Some small-animal veterinarians own large practices that generate considerable revenue. There are also very experienced individuals in high positions at dog food companies who earn six-figure salaries every year. But it's important to remember that these well-compensated individuals are the exception rather than the rule.

If you want to get rich working with dogs, you will have your job cut out for you. You'll need to pursue one of the higher paying professions, and develop a unique and dynamic plan to set yourself apart from everyone else in your field. Even then, there is no guarantee.

If your dream is to work with dogs, it is best to have the attitude that your rewards will come in forms other than financial. Knowing that you are helping dogs live a better life, and helping their owners to enjoy them more can be incredibly satisfying and can more than make up for a moderate paycheck.

Long Hours: If you want a profession with dogs, depending on the type of job you pursue, you may find yourself working more than the traditional forty-hour week. While some positions allow flexibility in the amount of time you put in (especially if you work for yourself), most are considerably demanding.

Much like their human equivalents in the health care professions, veterinarians, veterinary technicians, and veterinary assistants tend to put in long hours, since their jobs involve caring for sick animals. Professional handlers spend considerable time on the road going from dog show to dog show, and editors, attorneys, and marketing specialists rarely work eight-hour days.

There are some positions in the dog industry that are less demanding and, therefore, call for fewer hours. A groomer who works for a shop owner can prearrange an eight-hour-a-day working schedule, as can a kennel aide or retail assistant. However, more rewarding and better-paying situations tend to call for flexibility in the number of hours worked per day, as well as days worked per week. This is not to say that a job working with dogs means you won't have time for anything else in your life; it *does*

mean, however, that, in most instances, you won't be working strictly from nine to five.

ADVANTAGES

The Dogs: The most obvious advantage, and the reason you are even considering a canine career, is that your work will revolve around dogs. If your profession is in one of the hands-on careers, you will be surrounded by living, breathing, four-legged creatures whose happy expressions and affectionate behavior will bring you joy each and every day. If you are working in a job where there are no actual dogs, but dogs are the subject, the rewards are nearly as great. There is nothing worse than having to immerse yourself daily in a subject you care little about. If you truly love dogs, the acts of thinking and talking about them all day long can be incredibly enriching. When all your creative energy is being focused on a topic you are passionate about, job satisfaction is high.

Social Rewards: Have you ever noticed that people are friendlier to you when you are walking with a dog at your side than when you are without one? There is something about the presence of a dog that breaks social barriers and encourages people to open up to one another. This is true not only on the sidewalk but also in the workplace.

Whether it is the unconditional love that dogs give or simply their willingness to often happily greet people they hardly know, dogs bring out the best in us. Whether you are working in a veterinary office, a grooming shop, a marketing department, or a law office, people working in dog-related professions will most likely be happier and friendlier than people in nondoggy environments.

In addition to providing you with a pleasant workplace, working in a dog-oriented profession will also allow you to meet other people with the same canine passion that you have. You will make friends more easily and will share a common bond with nearly everyone you work with.

Knowledge: People who love dogs want to know as much about them as possible, and there are few things more educational than a career immersed in these charming animals.

Not only will you learn about dogs during the educational process required to prepare you for your work, but you will continue to learn throughout your career. Dogs provide so much opportunity for discovery, and the people who work with them are constantly unearthing new bits of information about their charges.

Dogs also have a way of teaching us about ourselves. Just being in their presence enriches not only our minds, but also our souls.

MARKETING YOURSELF

CHOOSING THE RIGHT JOB

You love dogs and you want to spend the rest of your life working with them. But what *exactly* do you want to do? Figuring this part out can be difficult. There are so many different career options. Maybe you are drawn to all of them. Or perhaps you like the way some of them sound, but aren't sure which one would be best suited to your skills.

It may be daunting to look at the long list of career choices in this book and then try to figure out the best one for you. But don't let the task of deciding your professional future frighten or discourage you. With the right attitude, you can actually make this part of the process a lot of fun. Think of your career life as an empty scrapbook, and you now get to decide what kinds of wonderful experiences will be lining its pages someday.

FINDING YOURSELF

Picking a profession is a very personal task, something that only you can decide for yourself. Your friends and family can give you suggestions about what they *think* you will be good at, but only you know what feels right. Deciding what you will do for the rest of your life requires a lot of soul searching and close examination of yourself. It is within your own heart and mind that you will find the answer to what is the best job for you.

Begin by thinking about what matters to you most in life. We already know a little bit about you. Most likely, you are considering a career with dogs because you're the kind of person who wants to feel emotionally connected to what you want to do for a living. Some people base their career decision on how much money they will make, others on what kind of status a job will give them. Others pick a profession based on the career traditions of their family, while still more go into a field simply because an opportunity fell into their lap. You, on the other hand, have a passion for dogs and want to work with them. That puts you in a league of your own. You are a person whose career objectives and emotions are closely aligned. Therefore, when you make your decision, you must follow your heart.

Take a look at the different careers presented in this book, and read through the job descriptions, as well as the advantages and disadvantages. Then go out and learn as much as you possibly can about the jobs that interest you. Read articles on the subject, contact the professional organization that represents each career, and spend some time watching professionals at their work. Use the Internet too. The dog community has a strong presence on the World Wide Web, and information on various canine careers can be obtained here by using one of the many "search engines" available to Internet "surfers."

As you study each profession, monitor your feelings closely. Which one do you easily envision yourself doing? Which one seems most closely aligned with who you really are? Imagine yourself doing this for a living. Does this picture of yourself make you feel excited and happy? Would you be proud to tell people that this was your career? Could you see yourself in this position day in and day out, year after year? How you respond to the above questions is the most important criteria you will have in determining which career is best for you.

Another way to narrow your job choice is to look closely at your personality traits and individual skills. What kinds of things are you good at? Are you proficient at science and math? Are you an analytical type of person with a penchant for nurturing? Do you enjoy going to school? If you answered yes to these questions, you might be suited to a career in the veterinary health field.

On the other hand, maybe you are someone who enjoys art. You like to paint or sculpt in your spare time, and your friends often come to you for a between-haircuts trim. When it comes to dogs, you find yourself fascinated by the many different coat types that are out there. You love the sight and smell of a freshly groomed dog. If this sounds like you, you are a good candidate for a career as a groomer.

This type of personal assessment can be applied to any of the many dog-related jobs that are out there. If you love to read, write, and organize things, you may be suited to being a dog magazine editor. If you enjoy debating and studying and find yourself fascinated by the legal system, a career as an attorney specializing in canine subjects may be in your future. Take a close look at who you are, what you like to do, and why you like to do it, and apply these traits to any of the jobs listed in this book. You may not find a career that matches your skills exactly (you may love science but can't stand the sight of blood), but with a little open-mindedness, you can find something that feels right for you.

GETTING PREJOB EXPERIENCE

 One of the most frustrating things about the work world is that you often need job experience in order to get job experience. This is true whether you are embarking on a career as an accountant or an animal-welfare advocate. People who are looking to hire a new employee want to see that you have done some of this kind of work before they give you a chance with their firm. Yet, how are you supposed to ever get that experience if no one will ever hire you without it? This problem doesn't just apply to canine careers. All professionals must deal with the difficulties of trying to get work experience when they don't yet have any. It's just the way of the world.

The good news is that people who want to work with dogs will find it easier to solve this problem than those who are seeking futures in other professions. The reason for this is simple: because of the hobby nature of the dog world, there are a lot more opportunities out there to get hands-on experience working with dogs. And that hands-on experience can help you get your foot in the professional door.

Volunteering: Prejob experience in many cases means volunteering, something many dog lovers already do. If you are interested in working in the animal control profession, spend a few hours a week helping out at your local animal shelter. If you want to be a professional dog writer or photographer, offer to provide articles and photographs to a breed or local club newsletter. If you want to be a veterinary assistant, contact a small-animal vet in your area and ask if you can help clean cages. All of these tasks are experiences that you can list on your resumé. When a prospective employer is weighing your qualifications, this volunteer experience will go a long way. It will also give you a chance to get a closer look at the profession you are considering and help you decide if this is what you really want to do.

Internships: Another way to gain experience in the field you have chosen is through educational internships. Many schools, both trade and professional, offer students the opportunity to get hands-on experience through internships. Sometimes the internships are paid, but in most cases, students do the work in exchange for educational credits. In many situations, the internship turns into a full-time job once the student has finished his education.

If the career you choose requires formal schooling and you have not yet had the opportunity to gain hands-on experience in the area you wish to work, try to enroll in a college or school that offers regular internships to its students. If you choose a career like marketing or editorial work, it's unlikely you will find an internship that relates directly to dogs. Don't pass it up, however. This nondoggy internship combined with your extracurricular canine activities will make you especially qualified for an entry-level job in a dog-focused company.

Working: Another way to gain experience in your chosen field is to take a part-time position, even though you are really looking for full-time work. Part-time jobs are sometimes initially easier to find than full-time jobs, but these part-time positions often become full-time work over time.

Even the part-time jobs that don't turn into full-time work are of great value in terms of gaining experience. It's much easier to find a full-time position once you have done the same job part-time. If you can find a part-time job while you are attending school, all the better. This will not only help you gain valuable experience, but will also show future employers that you are highly motivated. Earning money to attend school while also working on your education comes across as a big plus to many employers.

GETTING YOUR FOOT IN THE DOOR

Probably the most difficult part of starting a new career is getting that first break. It can sometimes be hard to find the right position and convince a potential employer to give you a chance at the job. Every person starting out in a career faces this dilemma, but it is a rare individual who doesn't eventually get that break.

There are a number of different ways to get your foot in the door of a new career. By using some or even all of the following methods, you will get your opportunity to shine.

Networking: Knowing what you want to do and having the right education and/or experience are vital when it comes to getting your first break in a new profession. But probably the most important way to get there is through networking. Who you know in the dog world and within your future profession will make a big difference in the kind of job you get—and how easily you get it.

What is networking, exactly? Many career books portray networking as a calculated effort to meet as many people as you can within your chosen profession. Although networking can legitimately be described in this way, it is less intimidating to think of it as socializing with people that share your same professional interests.

In some of the larger cities, helping people network has become a career in and of itself. Mixers held at local nightclubs are organized by those in the "networking profession," and social events sponsored by professional organizations are planned specifically with networking in mind.

For many people, this type of formal networking feels forced and uncomfortable. Walking into a room full of strangers and trying to make conversation that will help further careers can be nerve-wracking, or even frightening. But there are other, better ways to network, and the dog world is perfect for these.

If you are already involved with dogs, whether it be showing them, doing volunteer work on their behalf, or just taking yours to the local dog park, you are already one step ahead of the game. The people you have met while participating in these activities are your first network contacts. More than likely, you have become friendly with some of them (the ones you really like), and they already know you by name. When you are ready to start looking for your first job, all you need to do is let them know that you are seeking a position as a groomer, an obedience instructor, or a pet supplies marketing specialist. They themselves may not be doing those jobs, but chances are they know someone who is. This is especially true of people in the purebred dog show world, who tend to be very involved with their dogs and know many people in the dog-related professions.

Volunteering in a place where dogs are found is another good way to network, especially if you can find a group or activity that is closely related to what you want to do. If you want to be a professional handler, for example, offer your services to your local all-breed kennel club. Help them organize a match show, club dinner, or some other event. Here you will meet people who know professional handlers personally and can introduce you to them. Put the word out that you are looking for a position as an assistant to a pro, and you just might find that special job you are looking for.

Once you get your first professional job, don't stop networking. In most cases, it will come naturally as you meet people who do the same thing you do. You will find yourself becoming friends with some of these individuals, and acquaintances with many more. If you tend to be a quiet and reserved person, make a concerted effort to get to know those around you. Build yourself an ongoing network of fellow professionals; these people will help you for the rest of your career life. They can be your key to future jobs and even detailed information on potential employers you may be considering. There is no substitute in the professional world for a good network—something you will soon learn as you make your way through your career.

School Placement: One of the benefits of choosing a dog-related career that requires a formal education is access to the school placement office. Whether you are attending a trade school to become a dog trainer or a university to become a marketing specialist, there will probably be job placement services available to you.

In colleges and universities, placement offices network within the professional community to ferret out entry-level jobs for new graduates. Students can register with the job placement office and receive information on jobs that are available. Some schools even offer assistance in making the initial contact and setting up the interview.

Trade schools offer job placement services as well, providing students with job leads in their field. This is often an excellent way to find that first job that will get you started in your new profession.

Published Jobs: This is probably the most difficult way to find a dog-related job, especially if you plan to rely only on your local newspaper for employment listings. While it's not impossible to find a job with dogs in this way, it will be like looking for a needle in a haystack. You should take the time to study your Sunday employment classifieds in the event that a dog-related job might turn up, but don't make this your only means of searching.

Certain canine careers are supported by professional organizations, many of which produce a regular publication devoted strictly to this career. Job listings can often be found in these magazines and newspapers. Contact the appropriate organization and find out how you can subscribe. You may also want to consider joining the organization itself, since this will not only garner you a subscription to the group's publication, but may offer some networking opportunities as well.

Dog magazines are another place where jobs are listed, usually in the classified sections. The problem with searching for a job this way is that the listings will most likely be for positions outside of your immediate geographical area. Unless you are willing to move, you may not be able to locate a position that is suitable to you.

Word of Mouth: This goes back to networking. If you know people in the dog community, you should put the word out that you are looking for a job. You can also try contacting veterinary offices and other professionals in the pet industry to ask if they are aware of any job openings in your field. Many jobs are filled in this way, because a great majority of positions are never even advertised.

Employment Agencies: Entry-level jobs can sometimes be obtained with the help of employment agencies. In this day and age, however, employment agencies have become very specialized. You will need to do some searching for an agency that places people in your field of choice. You won't find any agencies that specialize in dog careers, but you will find some that place lawyers, marketers, and editors. If you feel strongly about making your first job in one of these professions dog-related, you can specify this to the representative who works with you at the agency. Don't expect to get any calls if your search is that narrow, however. Dog-related jobs in this field are few and far between and rarely come through job agencies.

Cold Calling: Normally, this approach is not a very successful way to find a job. However, if you are specializing in a dog-related career, it's not a bad way to go. Entry level groomers, for example, can make a list of every grooming shop in their area and call each one to find out if they are looking for a new hire. Recent graduates who want to specialize in public relations for a dog food company would be wise to contact the people in charge of the public relations departments of the major dog food manufacturers. Because a career with dogs is so specialized and because there are a limited number of employers in each canine field, cold calling can often be a good way of letting the powers-that-be know that you are out there.

THAT IMPORTANT PAPERWORK

Knowing the right people can help you find out about that dream job. Studying the want ads is another way that prospective applicants learn about positions with dogs. But in order to get that all-important interview, you need to present something on paper that will convince the employer that you are especially qualified for the job.

Resumés: Many books have been written on the preparation of resumés, and there are a lot of different ways to present your qualifications on paper. While the style and format you use is a matter of individual style, there are some vital points that you'll need to keep in mind when putting together this veritable calling card.

- Your most important qualifications should be listed first. If you have little on-the-job experience but a degree specifically related to the job you are seeking, put your education first. If you have worked for a period of time as a volunteer in the same or related position you are seeking, list that at the top of your resumé.

- Don't minimize the amount of personal time you have spent with dogs, because this is important to your qualifications. If your paid work experience is short on dog-related material, be sure to include a section on your resumé called "Volunteer Activities." Here you can tell employers about your nonpaid work with canines. If you don't have any volunteer work in your background, list your experience with dogs under "Hobbies." Employers in most dog-related careers will be looking for some hands-on familiarity with dogs. Listing your dog as one of your hobbies will let the person reviewing your resumé know that you have a strong interest in and knowledge of dogs.

- Keep your resumé down to one page if possible. If you are having trouble doing this, remember to only list the education and experience that is most relevant to the job you are trying to land.

- Double-check your resumé after you have finished to make sure there are no grammatical or typographical errors. Resumés serve as a first impression to potential employers, and you need to put forth a conscientious and organized image. These are two important qualities for people who want to work with dogs.

Cover Letters: Every resumé must be accompanied by a cover letter. The cover letter provides a more personal touch to the resumé and helps capture the attention of the person responsible for doing the hiring.

When writing your cover letter, follow these recommendations:

- Find out who will be reading your resumé, and address the cover letter directly to this person.

- Early on in the letter, be sure to mention the name of the contact or referral person who told you about the job. Associating yourself with a person familiar to the reader can set you apart from all the other applicants.

- Use the cover letter as an opportunity to stress your dog-related and other relevant experience. Even though it already appears in your resumé, it doesn't hurt to point it out one more time.

- At the end of your letter, be sure to request a job interview. List a telephone number where you can be easily reached or where prospective employers can leave messages for you.

THE INTERVIEW

 Whereas the resumé and cover letter are important, the interview itself is usually the determining factor in whether or not you will get the job. Employers use interviews not only to determine the skills of the person applying for the position, but also the applicant's personality and enthusiasm for the job.

Interviewing can be an anxiety-provoking experience. The notion of being evaluated in a situation where the future of your career will be determined by the outcome leaves many people quivering in anticipatory fear. While it's natural to be nervous during an interview, don't let your nerves overwhelm you. Try to focus on presenting your skills to your prospective employer and on learning more about the job at hand. What many interviewees don't realize is that they are also evaluating the employer—not just vice versa. Employers want to impress job candidates nearly as much as the candidates want to impress them. Keep this in mind when you are sitting across from someone you would like to work with. Just be yourself.

Following are some important elements to bring out in your job interview:

- Learn as much as you can about the company or place you are interviewing with *before* you arrive for your interview. Showing the prospective employer that you know something about the firm will impress him. Also, if you can find out what kinds of problems the company has and diplomatically suggest that you can help solve some of these problems if you are hired, you will be even closer to getting the job.

- Talk a lot about your experience with dogs. Not only will this show the employer that you have a great interest and knowledge of the canine species, it will also create a bond between the two of you. People who love dogs share something very profound in common, and this is the kind of connection you want to nurture with the individual responsible for making the hiring decision.

- Be prepared to ask questions about the job itself. While the prospective employer is evaluating you, this is your chance to evaluate the job. Find out exactly what your duties will be, what kind of hours you will be expected to work, and how much the salary is. As the interview goes along, more questions will undoubtedly pop into your head. Feel free to ask them as long as they aren't questions that will put forth any negative feelings you may be having about the job. Your goal is to get a job offer. It will then be up to you whether you want to accept or decline.

- Dress professionally. Even if you are applying for a job that will require you to spend most of your time cleaning kennel runs, a neat, professional appearance will give the employer a good first impression. Wear a business suit, if possible. This type of apparel will say to the employer that you are professional, serious about your work, and respectful of his establishment.

- Always follow up your interview with a thank-you note. An informal note can mean the difference between getting the job and missing out. Tell the employer that you enjoyed meeting him, that you are very enthusiastic about the job, and that you hope you will be chosen for the position. Human nature being what it is, this is often the deciding factor for many employers who are looking for just the right employee.

HEALTH CARE PROFESSIONS

One of the highest paying and most rewarding professions for people who love dogs is veterinary medicine. Veterinarians are among the most respected and admired of all pet professionals, and it's no wonder. The veterinarian's job is to save the lives of our beloved pets, to ease the pain of these innocent animals, and to make the quality of their lives better. Dog owners often look up to their pet's veterinarian as someone very important and very special.

Veterinary technicians and assistants, while not as well paid or recognized as the veterinarians they work for, still reap many of the rewards that come with a job in a veterinary-related profession. They are an integral part of the daily workings of veterinary offices and hospitals everywhere, sharing in both the ups and downs that come with any involvement in the exciting world of medicine.

POSITION: VETERINARIAN

 Let's begin our look at the canine health care professions with the top job, that of veterinarian. There are approximately 60,000 veterinarians practicing in the United States today. When we hear the word "veterinarian," we usually think of the man or woman who works at the local veterinary clinic and provides our dog with its annual vaccines and cares for it when it is sick. Although this is the most visible side of veterinary medicine, there are many other aspects of the job as well. Veterinarians perform a number of different functions, all relating to the health of dogs, cats, and other animals.

The career outlook for veterinarians is excellent. Studies show that 100 percent of veterinary school graduates find work related to their field or go on to pursue graduate degrees in veterinary medicine. Job security is one of the best reasons to become a veterinarian.

DUTIES

The everyday tasks performed by a veterinarian depend on the type of career paths he has chosen. There are several different types of veterinarians who work with dogs. Known as small-animal veterinarians, these medical professionals have the option of choosing a traditional career in private practice, a corporate career working for a large company, or a career in veterinary research, regulatory veterinary medicine, or military veterinary medicine. Each of these jobs employs the use of veterinary medicine, but each is very different from the other.

The most traditional role for veterinarians is that of private practitioner. The majority of practicing veterinarians do this type of work.

The responsibilities of the private practitioner are many. Depending on her position in the practice, this person is responsible for examining both cats and dogs, as well as other animals; making diagnoses; administering medications and vaccines; assisting in surgery; cleaning teeth; and performing euthanasia. Many veterinarians, particularly those who are just getting started, will work for a more experienced veterinarian who owns the practice. Considered a staff veterinarian, this newcomer will be on the practice payroll and earn a regular salary, often with periodic bonuses, and commissions for emergency after-hours work.

Corporate veterinarians, on the other hand, have a very different job. Unlike traditional veterinarians, they don't deal with pet owners directly, but instead provide their expertise to the corporations for which they work. Corporate veterinarians are usually involved in the research and development of new products, including vaccines, medications, and nutritional products. They are employed by pharmaceutical firms, dog food companies, and manufacturers of dog-related items.

While many corporate veterinarians spend most of their time in the laboratory working on product development, others function in more of a marketing capacity. Their job is to present the veterinary products to potential customers, usually retailers or veterinarians in private practice.

Research veterinarians can be found plying their trade at the many veterinary universities in the United States and Canada. Here they strive to find cures to the many debilitating canine diseases that plague our four-footed friends. Many of these veterinary researchers also go on to become professors, teaching future veterinarians the intricacies of their profession.

Some research veterinarians prefer to work in the human medical field, where they conduct research on animals in order to discover the causes and cures of illnesses that affect humans. Many people who want to become veterinarians because they have a strong love and empathy for dogs tend to stay away from this area of veterinary medicine since it requires compromising the well-being of individual dogs for research purposes relating to humans.

Regulatory and military veterinarians work for the government, using their skills and knowledge for a variety of purposes relating to animals used by the Defense Department. Military veterinarians are enlisted members of the armed forces.

WHAT IT TAKES

In order to become successful as a veterinarian, you will need to be in possession of some very distinctive personality traits. Let's assume you already love animals (not just dogs, but other animals too) and want to help them. These are vital requirements if you want to be a vet, but there is more to it than just that.

First, you have to be a highly motivated person. Learning to become a vet and then working as one is hard, and if you don't want it badly enough, you won't be able to pull it off. Veterinary school is very demanding, requiring long hours of study and many weeks of uninterrupted and difficult academic work with little time for recreational activities. Once you are out of school, you'll find that veterinary work itself can also be taxing. Most small-animal vets work at least 50 hours a week, while some put in a lot more time than that. Veterinarians in private practice without emergency backup often find themselves working in the middle of the night, on holidays, and on weekends.

In order to be a vet, you also need brain power. Math and science are two subjects in which prospective veterinarians must excel. A great deal of veterinary school curriculum will consist of these topics, and the material you learn must be retained and applied to real-life situations later on.

Good people skills are another prerequisite for being a veterinarian, especially if you plan to go into private practice. While much of your time will be spent with dogs and other animals, a lot of it will also involve dealing with owners as well. In fact, your success as a veterinarian will hinge, in large part, on your "bedside manner." Pet owners not only judge veterinarians by how well these professionals practice medicine but also by how comfortable the vet makes them feel.

In order to be successful as a veterinarian, you must also have a desire to work with animals as a medical scientist. While an affection for animals is present in many veterinarians, so is a passion for medicine. Being a vet isn't just about handling dogs—it's about studying the diseases that plague them, and trying to conquer these diseases.

ADVANTAGES

There are many advantages to being a veterinarian. One is the amount of money you earn, although it's important to realize that most veterinarians don't get rich. They make a comfortable living but not nearly as much as human doctors or even professionals in other fields.

Respect in society, particularly within the animal community, is a huge benefit of being a veterinarian. Pet owners, breeders, and trainers will look up to you if you are a veterinarian. Most will value your opinion and follow your advice like gospel.

One of the most obvious advantages of being a veterinarian is the chance to work with animals—especially dogs—on a daily basis. The opportunity to help animals in distress and to see the positive results of your efforts can make all your efforts worthwhile.

DISADVANTAGES

There are several disadvantages to being a veterinarian. First, it's not easy to become one. Four years of specialized schooling beyond undergraduate college is required, and the course work is difficult. It's also expensive. Most veterinary students have to borrow money to pay their way through school and spend around 10 years after they graduate paying off the debt. This can be somewhat of a hardship because entry-level veterinary positions are not very high paying.

The difficulty of veterinary school is good practice for the job itself, which often requires working in the middle of the night on emergency cases, on holidays, and even on weekends. Veterinarians also face the hazards of being bitten by a frightened or aggressive animal.

Unfortunately, a big part of a veterinarian's job is euthanizing animals. Many of these are dogs that are old and sick, but there are quite a few that are not. There are homeless animals and those that have been injured or become ill because of owners who simply don't care. These are all difficult situations you will have to deal with if you become a veterinarian. This aspect of the profession is one of the hardest to cope with.

There's also the helpless feelings vets experience when they lose a patient. Being in charge of an animal's life is a huge responsibility, and when all your efforts fail and the animal dies anyway, it can be tremendously difficult.

EDUCATION

Of all the careers with dogs that one could choose, a career in veterinary medicine requires the most schooling, with your education beginning even before you enter a veterinary college. Before you can apply to vet school, you must be a high school graduate, and before you attend veterinary school, you must complete your prerequisite undergraduate work.

Although it is not necessary to obtain a four-year degree before applying to veterinary school, having one will greatly increase your chances of being accepted. Choose a major like biology or animal science for your undergraduate degree—something that will include all the prerequisite classes required by the veterinary school you want to apply to.

Regardless of whether or not you earn a bachelor's degree, you will need to take all the prerequisites called for by the veterinary college that you plan to attend. For this reason, it's important to choose a veterinary school early on. If there's a veterinary college in the state or province where you live, you should consider this one first, because tuition is usually lower and admission is usually easier for residents. All of the veterinary colleges in the United States and Canada have programs in small-animal medicine in their curriculums. However, you should take a close look at the faculty expertise of the school you are thinking about attending, particularly if you plan to go on to specialize in an area, such as surgery, cardiology, or anesthesiology after you graduate. Check into the active research projects and faculty expertise of the school before you make a commitment.

It's also a good idea to make an appointment with an advisor at each of the schools you are considering so you can get advice on your preveterinary education, as well as pay a visit to the campus. You will be spending a lot of time at the college you will eventually enter, and the more comfortable you feel there, the better you will do.

Another prerequisite for entrance into veterinary school is hands-on experience with animals, preferably in a medical setting. As you attend undergraduate school, seek out as much experience with dogs and other animals as you can. If you can get a job with a local veterinarian, do it. If you can't find paying work, volunteer for the summer. Do whatever you can to spend time working or helping out in a veterinary environment. The people scrutinizing your application in the admissions office at the veterinary college will be looking for this experience. They want to be sure you know something firsthand about the profession you are entering.

Once you have chosen a veterinary college, completed the prerequisites, and gained experience working with animals, you are ready to apply to veterinary school. Admission to veterinary school has become very competitive in recent years; only 35.7 percent of those who applied for admission in 1996 were accepted. Of all the veterinary colleges in the United States, only 2,111 students graduated that year. With these kinds of statistics, it's obvious that only those students with the highest grade point averages and the best animal experience make it into and through veterinary school.

Aside from gaining acceptance, one of the biggest considerations when applying to veterinary school is finance. Tuition is not cheap, and the majority of students need some type of financial aid to pay for their education. In fact, approximately 75 percent of veterinary students depend on federally subsidized loans.

While the primary responsibility for financing a veterinary education rests with the student, there are a number of programs that are administered by the government to assist those who cannot afford to pay their tuition up front. Some of these programs allow students to work on campus to earn part of their tuition; others allow students to borrow significant amounts of money to get through school. Be careful to borrow wisely, however. An excessive debt will be difficult or impossible to start paying back on a veterinarian's entry-level salary.

GETTING A JOB

Once you have the title of Doctor of Veterinary Medicine after your name (or Veterinary Medical Doctor, in the case of University of Pennsylvania graduates), a whole world of opportunity will be open for you. You will be prepared to start work as a practicing veterinarian.

There are a number of ways to go about getting your first veterinary position. The classified sections of veterinary journals list positions around the country that are available. Or, you may learn of a position through your veterinary college. You may even have been lucky enough to secure an internship after your final year of study, and this position may become a permanent job.

If you want to go into private practice, it's likely that your first job will be working at a veterinary clinic under the supervision of one or more experienced veterinarians. Here you will have an opportunity to learn the profession firsthand and will be able to confer with vets who have been practicing for some time. You will learn a tremendous amount in this situation and eventually will know enough to move out on your own.

SALARY

Annual salaries for new veterinarians practicing small-animal medicine begin around $32,000 and rapidly increase over the first five years of practice. A typical veterinarian in private practice plateaus at $60,000 to $70,000. Vets who go on to work in medical research and in corporate environments can earn considerably more.

POSITION: VETERINARY TECHNICIAN

Working right alongside veterinarians in private practice, laboratories, veterinary hospitals, zoos, and even animal shelters are veterinary technicians. Functioning as the right-hand person to a busy doctor, the veterinary technician is responsible for providing much of the medical care administered in veterinary hospitals today. Veterinary technicians are the registered nurses of the animal world.

DUTIES

There are a number of responsibilities that veterinary technicians take on as part of their role. Preparing animals and the operating room for surgery is one of these jobs, as are disinfecting the surgery room and instruments, wound management, and performing other presurgery-related functions. Assisting in the surgery is another part of the technician's job and can include handing instruments to the doctor during the operation and monitoring the heart rate and respiration of the patient, as well as other functions. Providing care for the postoperative animal is also the technician's work.

Most veterinary clinics employ one or more veterinary technicians to aid in the daily care of hospitalized patients. This calls for feeding, administering medications, gathering samples, physical therapy, bandage and dressing application, nutritional management, bathing, and even cleaning cages. It also requires a watchful eye as many veterinarians depend heavily on their technicians to monitor the health of the animals in their care.

Cleaning teeth, anesthesiology, radiology (the taking of x-rays), and certain aspects of clinic pathology may also be performed by the veterinary technician.

Not all of the technician's duties involve only animals. Face-to-face contact with pet owners is a large part of the job. At many veterinary hospitals, the technician is the first person the pet owner talks to about the health of the pet. Technicians will sometimes take down the history of the pet before the doctor sees it and ask questions about the health of the animal.

Some technicians in smaller clinics are also responsible for clerical duties like medical supplies inventory control, bookkeeping, filing, and answering the phone. Most veterinarians prefer to hire a veterinary assistant to do this type of work so the technicians can spend their time working directly with patients, but not all practices are big enough to afford this luxury. Consequently, veterinarian technicians in AVMA (American Veterinary Medical Association) accredited programs are taught these office management functions.

WHAT IT TAKES

It takes a special kind of person to become a veterinary technician. The technician's job is multifaceted and calls for a number of different personality traits and skills.

One of the most important things you need to be a successful veterinary technician is a concern and compassion for animals. The majority of your job will consist of contact with sick and injured animals, creatures that are frightened and suffering. You must be able to empathize with these animals and have patience with them, since pets in these situations are sometimes difficult to handle.

Brain power is another requirement of the veterinary technician. The technician is expected to know and understand medical ideas and concepts and to be proficient in the anatomy and body systems of a number of different animal species. Special schooling is required to be a veterinary technician, and science and math classes in these programs are par for the course.

Like the veterinarian, the technician who works in a private practice must have good people skills. Technicians in these jobs spend a lot of time dealing with pet owners, and they must like people if they are going to be happy in this work. Empathy for humans is a good trait for veterinary technicians to possess because they will deal with people who are nearly as frightened and upset as the animals themselves.

The ability to take direction is another mandatory trait for the veterinary technician. By definition, the technician's job is to assist the veterinarian. This means cheerfully following the instructions given to you by the person who is above you in both rank and education. If you don't like the idea of being told what to do, this isn't the job for you.

ADVANTAGES

Veterinary technicians get to work with dogs day in and day out, and this is probably the job's greatest reward. For people who love the idea of not only spending time with animals but also helping them at the same time, there is no better career than that of veterinary technician.

Veterinary technicians report that being part of a pet's success story is tremendously gratifying. When a sick or injured pet is made well, and you know that you were an integral part of that care, there is a great feeling of satisfaction.

Another bonus for veterinary technicians is the opportunity to work closely with veterinarians. If you are the kind of person who loves to learn on a constant basis, working side-by-side with a veterinarian every day will be a real treat for you. In this position, you will learn an incredible amount about the science of veterinary medicine and will have the chance to spend time with other people who share the same interest.

DISADVANTAGES

The greatest disadvantage to being a veterinary technician is the pay. Compared to veterinarians, technicians make a very small salary, sometimes not even enough to pay their bills. Most veterinary technicians find that they have to share living space with another person in order to make ends meet or have a spouse who earns considerably more.

To make the matter of low pay even worse, veterinary technicians often have to work long hours, on weekends, and on holidays. This varies from situation to situation, but most clinics require their veterinary technicians to put in time on the weekends and during after-hour emergencies.

On the emotional side, veterinary technicians have to deal with the constant pain and suffering they see among the animals that they so dearly love. It can be taxing on your emotions to come to work every day when you know you will be seeing a certain amount of anguish and death that you will feel helpless to alleviate.

There's also the very real possibility that you could end up being bitten by a frightened or aggressive animal.

EDUCATION

In order to become a veterinary technician, you must go to school. There are a few options here, depending on what your educational preferences are.

Most veterinary technicians attend a two-year college in order to obtain an Associate of Applied Science degree designed especially for this career. This can be a private college or a community college, preferably with a program accredited by the AVMA. (A list of accredited colleges in the United States can be obtained by contacting the AVMA [see appendix]). Students in these programs learn anatomy, chemistry, behavior, surgical procedure, pharmacology, and more.

Some people who become veterinary technicians earn a four-year degree in biology, animal science, or zoology. The benefit to earning a bachelor's degree is that you can go on to other careers or even a higher education with this degree. Some veterinary technicians go on to become veterinarians, and those with four-year degrees have a greater chance of acceptance into veterinary school.

Extracurricular activities with animals can also enrich your education as a veterinary technician. Volunteer work at an animal shelter or part-time work at any place that houses animals is a good bet.

Upon completion of your formal education as a veterinary technician, you will want to take an accrediting exam with the State Board of Veterinary Examiners or whichever agency is responsible for certifying, licensing, or registering veterinary technicians in your area. Currently, forty states and provinces monitor veterinary technicians and test them for competency through an exam. Having a board-certified accreditation will help you get the best job possible.

GETTING A JOB

There are a couple of ways to get your first job as a veterinary technician once you have earned either your two-year or four-year degree and your accreditation. Utilize the job placement service at your college, if there is one. You can also start calling all the veterinary hospitals and clinics in your area to find out if they are accepting applications.

Scan your local newspaper as well. Veterinary technician jobs are often listed in the classified section under "animal care" and "veterinary."

SALARY

Veterinary technicians make anywhere from $7 to $10 an hour to start, depending on what part of the country you live in and what kind of place you work. Smaller clinics and one-vet practices typically pay the lowest, and larger hospitals and research labs are in the upper areas of the salary range.

Salaries tend to top at $15 an hour, even for the most experienced technicians.

POSITION: VETERINARY ASSISTANT

There is a fine line between the job of veterinary assistant and veterinary technician. In fact, in some private practices, there is no distinction between the two. However, in most places, the veterinary technician provides more hands-on service in the medical areas of the practice, and the veterinary assistant deals primarily with phones and paperwork.

DUTIES

Some veterinary assistants are able to assist in surgery, give baths, and do some of the work that a technician would do. Most, however, are responsible for helping the veterinarian run his practice.

When you go to your veterinarian's office with your pet, it is a veterinary assistant who first greets you. This person is the one who scheduled your appointment, asked you to fill out a questionnaire on your pet, and pointed you to the examining room. The assistant also answers the telephone, files pet history folders, sends out billings, opens the mail, and does all the other routine office work that the veterinarian has no time to do.

Many veterinary assistants are also required to clean cages at veterinary hospitals and perform some other routine animal care procedures.

WHAT IT TAKES

In order to be happy working as a veterinary assistant, you must be content with a job that is essentially a support position. You won't be making important decisions regarding the health and well-being of pets, but you will be part of a team that makes this happen.

Because a big part of a veterinary assistant's job is talking to pet owners, a genuine interest in and empathy for people is needed to do well in this job. Many pet owners are under a great deal of stress when they bring their sick or injured pet to the veterinarian's office, and kind, careful treatment by the veterinary assistant can mean a great deal.

Emotional strength is also a necessary part of this job for the same reason. Veterinary assistants must be able to cope with the grief of owners who have lost their pets, and this can be a difficult part of the job.

Because veterinary assistants deal with important paperwork, a propensity to be organized and meticulous is a valuable trait in a person with this job. Good spelling, accurate typing, and general computer skills are also worthwhile abilities.

ADVANTAGES

The advantages of being a veterinary assistant include the opportunity to work with dogs and other animals on a daily basis. If you like people, the constant contact you will have with the public is another benefit.

Spending your work time with people who have similar interests to your own is another bonus for veterinary assistants. In this job, you will work alongside veterinarians, technicians, and possibly other assistants, people whose passion and love for animals is as great as yours.

Knowing you are part of the team that has helped save a beloved pet from the ravages of an injury or disease is one of the greatest advantages of being a veterinary assistant. The smile on that grateful owner's face is worth its weight in gold.

DISADVANTAGES

The biggest disadvantage to being a veterinary assistant is the low salary. It's hard to make ends meet on what a veterinary assistant brings home every week. As a rule, assistants make even less than the technicians they work with.

Another disadvantage is the unpleasant sights that are a regular part of any veterinary practice. You will see pets that are sick, injured, and dying on a daily basis and will have to face the reality that a number of these patients just won't make it. This can be very hard for someone who loves animals.

Drudgery can sometimes be a problem for veterinary assistants who see the technicians and doctors in the practice dealing with life and death situations daily while all they do is answer phones and file paperwork. Although the assistant's job is important to the survival of the practice, assistants sometimes feel like the low guy on the totem pole.

EDUCATION

Veterinary assistants don't need more than a high school diploma or GED, although a certificate from a specialized trade school can be very helpful when trying to land that first job. Trade school programs for veterinary assistants teach the student basic animal care, office skills, and some veterinary subjects. They usually don't take more than one year to complete, and some can be earned through the mail.

GETTING A JOB

Finding a job as a veterinary assistant is similar to finding a position when you are a veterinary technician. If you attended a trade school for this career, utilize the institution's job placement services. Contact all the veterinary practices in your area to find out if they are accepting applications, and pursue any opening aggressively. Remember to also check the classified employment section of your Sunday paper for veterinary assistant positions.

SALARY

Veterinary assistants are paid by the hour, and start out at a wage of $5 to $7, depending on the area of the country and the size of the practice. Salary increases are small, incremental, and usually top out at around $12 for the most experienced assistants.

JOBS IN GENERAL DOG CARE

There's something about the act of making a dog's life happy and comfortable that is very rewarding. That's probably why most people who love dogs also enjoy caring for them.

If you think you like taking care of dogs so much that you might want to make a profession out of it, there are a few career possibilities you will want to consider. These include the jobs of boarding kennel owner-operator, kennel aide, and petsitter, all occupations born out of the idea that pet owners need someone to watch out for their animals while they are away. The jobs of boarding kennel owner-operator and petsitter are self-employed positions, something that attracts the entrepreneurial dog lover. The job of kennel aide is more traditional in that it involves working for someone else.

POSITION: BOARDING KENNEL OPERATOR

 If you like the idea of being around lots of animals, managing other people, and making good money, the job of boarding kennel owner-operator might be for you. Boarding kennel owner-operators are self-employed individuals who run their own facility with the help of one or more employees. Boarding kennels usually take in both dogs and cats and provide food, water, exercise, and regular supervision for these pets while their owners are out of town.

DUTIES

Boarding kennel owner-operators are first and foremost managers, people who oversee the pet care facility and run the daily business. They make sure the animals under their supervision are properly cared for. They also manage the employees who do much of the actual work (feeding, cleaning cages, administering necessary medications, and exercising pets). The boarding kennel owner-operator also deals directly with the pet owners who utilize her services.

Because the boarding kennel owner-operator is a small-business owner, she is also responsible for managing the books. This includes paying the bills, collecting boarding fees, and keeping the overhead down.

WHAT IT TAKES

In order to be a boarding kennel owner-operator, you need to not only love dogs, but you must like cats as well. Cats will make up a substantial portion of the pets who stay at your facility—unless you make your kennel a strictly "dogs only" operation. Although you can do this if you'd like, your pocketbook will miss those feline customers.

Because a good part of being a boarding kennel owner-operator is overseeing your kennel aides, you must be a good manager. You must know how to treat subordinates and how to get the most from them. A background in management is a huge asset here since directing people in the workplace can be a difficult and complicated task.

Good business sense is essential when running a boarding kennel. A background in business or experience managing any other kind of small company can be a huge help. You will need to raise capital to start your business, and your facility will need to be advertised, promoted, and marketed if it is to succeed.

The ability to deal well with the public is another important skill needed in a boarding kennel owner-operator. The way you handle yourself with your customers will make a big difference in whether or not they bring their pet back a second or third time. Whenever the public is concerned, patience, the ability to listen well, and a genuine like of people are good assets.

ADVANTAGES

If you are passionate about dogs, the clearest advantage to being a boarding kennel owner-operator is the chance to be around them every day and to know that you are providing them the best care you can until their owners return. This is a rewarding feeling for people who truly love animals.

Potential to earn a good living is another advantage to being a boarding kennel owner-operator. Your operation can be as small as you like or as big as you care to make it. The bigger kennels obviously bring in a lot more revenue than the smaller ones, but even a tiny operation can yield a comfortable salary for its owner.

Another huge benefit to being a boarding kennel owner-operator is the self-employment aspect. There are few things more wonderful in the professional world than being your own boss. You make the decisions, you make the rules. Everything functions in just the way you want it. There's no boss to listen to, no clock to punch. It's a wonderful feeling, one that few people want to give up once they've tried it—that is, of course, if they can deal with some of the disadvantages of self-employment.

DISADVANTAGES

There are several disadvantages that come with the job. One is the level of financial responsibility that goes along with any self-employed position. If business is bad, you will suffer personally. You may even have the unpleasant job of having to lay off your employees or borrow money against your home to keep the place going. This is a real possibility for any small business owner. Personally, you will also be responsible for paying for your own health insurance, and social security, disability, and self-employment taxes.

Even though you will have the freedom of being your own boss, you won't have the opportunity to come and go as you please. Because boarding kennels operate 7 days a week, 24 hours a day and are busiest during the holiday seasons, you will be committed to spending more time than you may want to at work.

In order to start a boarding facility, you will need a considerable amount of start-up money. This capital is necessary for you to buy or rent a place for your facility and purchase kennels, cleaning supplies, and other items.

Although you may have employees working for you, you will also have to roll up your sleeves and do much of the work yourself. Cleaning runs and cages is probably the biggest job at a boarding kennel, and chances are you will be doing plenty of it.

Another disadvantage of being a boarding kennel owner-operator arises from the fact that you are dealing with the public on a daily basis. Disputes over bills and other problems that arise are a fact of life for boarding kennel operators.

EDUCATION

No formal education is required to become a boarding kennel operator, although a two- or four-year college degree in business can be very helpful. Starting and running a successful small business takes skill and knowledge, and a good place to acquire some of that is through formal schooling.

It's also possible to get an education on operating a boarding kennel from the American Boarding Kennels Association (see appendix). The professional organization for the boarding kennel industry, the American Boarding Kennels Association, offers correspondence courses that can prepare you for the job ahead. Two levels for those not yet involved in the profession are offered: pet care technician and advanced pet care technician. Students in these programs learn the basics of animal behavior, customer relations, and kennel management.

Once you are already working as a boarding kennel operator, you can enroll in the American Boarding Kennels Association certification program for boarding kennel operators where your knowledge of the field will be improved and tested. If you successfully complete the program, you will receive American Boarding Kennels Association certification.

If you have never worked at a boarding kennel, you should do this before you start your own operation. The day to day, hands-on experience you will receive as an employee will provide an invaluable education for when you are running your own facility.

GETTING A JOB
Unlike many other positions in the pet industry, you don't need to put in an application somewhere to become a boarding kennel operator if you plan to own your own place. All you need is the capital to get started, a business plan, and a design for your kennel, if you are starting one from scratch. You'll need to aggressively advertise and promote your facility to bring in those first customers.

Boarding kennel owner-operators can earn anywhere from $50,000 a year to $300,000, depending on the size—and success—of the their operation.

POSITION: KENNEL AIDE

Taking care of a kennel full of dogs (and cats) is a big job, and somebody has to do it. This is where the kennel aide comes in. Responsible for the comfort and well-being of a number of animals, the kennel aide performs a very important function in the daily workings of the facility.

Kennel aides are employed at veterinary hospitals and boarding kennels, two places where dogs are temporarily housed, either while receiving medical treatment or while their owners are away.

DUTIES

The duties of a kennel aide are varied, but there is one function that stands out among the rest in terms of time spent: cleaning. A sanitary environment is of the utmost importance at any kennel, and it is the kennel aide's job to keep cages and kennel runs clean and disinfected.

Another task of the kennel aide is providing food and water to the residents of the facility. Pets that need medicating may be administered to by the kennel aide, particularly at a boarding kennel. If bathing is a service provided by the facility, the kennel aide may be asked to perform this duty. Exercising the dogs is also a part of the kennel aide's job.

The general supervision of the pets at a boarding facility usually falls to the kennel aide, who comes to know each individual pet. Animals that appear to be sick or unhappy should be noticed by the person in this position and in turn reported to the manager of the facility. An aide must also monitor the conditions of cages and kennel runs.

WHAT IT TAKES

If you want to be a kennel aide, a basic love and knowledge of animals is needed. You wouldn't be able to stand being around that many dogs and cats at once if you didn't like them and understand them a whole lot.

You must be the type of person who truly enjoys caring for animals, because this will be your primary reward on the job. And because most of your time will be spent cleaning up after other people's pets, you have to get some enjoyment out of the idea of keeping things immaculate—even if it only lasts a short while.

Kennel work can be physically demanding, and you must be in good shape to do this job. A healthy back is especially important since all that bending and stooping can wreak havoc with a troubled spine.

A bit of modesty is in order if you plan to be a kennel aide, because the work required in this job is not very glamorous. You won't impress a lot of people with this career choice. Choose it only if you will truly enjoy the work.

ADVANTAGES

Being a kennel aide has a few advantages, the biggest of which is the love and attention you will receive from the animals in your care. You will be temporarily replacing these pets' owners and, for the time being, you are the center of their universe.

Another benefit of being a kennel aide is the mental ease of the job. Cleaning and scrubbing cages and runs can be hard physical work, but it's not the type of job you mentally take home with you. Unlike some other professionals in the pet world, you won't find yourself laying in bed at night worrying about the ongoing burdens and responsibilities of your work.

This is also one of the few dog-related jobs you can have if you don't particularly enjoy working with people. Kennel aides have contact only with the animals they care for and the other employees at the kennel. Dealing with the public is usually left up to the managers of the facility.

DISADVANTAGES

The biggest disadvantage to being a kennel aide is the pay, which is terrible, and there's no getting around it. Since it's nearly impossible to survive independently on a kennel aide's salary, only individuals with other financial support can afford to take on this position.

Another disadvantage is that kennel work is *hard* work. It can be physically draining to clean kennels and cages all day long, day in and day out.

You may also have to work on weekends and even holidays, since the animals at boarding facilities need to be cared for seven days a week, all year long.

EDUCATION

Neither a high school diploma nor a GED is required for a job as a kennel aide, although it is recommended since some employers prefer high school graduates. Some experience caring for animals, even if it's only volunteer work, is helpful for preparing prospective kennel aides for the job that lies ahead.

To increase your chances of getting a job as a kennel aide, you may want to consider enrolling in one or both of the American Boarding Kennels Association's education programs. Correspondence courses that teach the basics in animal behavior and pet care can look good on your resumé and show potential employers that you are serious about the job.

GETTING A JOB

Finding a job as a kennel aide requires calling boarding kennels and veterinary hospitals in your area and inquiring about the acceptance of resumés. Scanning the employment section of your local paper may turn up a position as well.

SALARY

The salary for a kennel aide usually begins at minimum wage. With a job well done, incremental raises can be gained, but the hourly wage will always remain small.

POSITION: PETSITTER

 In today's busy world, people need someone to help them take care of their pets. The scenarios vary. A family is going on vacation for two weeks and can't bring the animals with them. Or, a single person works an eight-hour day, and spends two hours a day commuting, leaving the dog home alone all day.

This is where the petsitter comes in. Petsitting is a relatively new career, a job that was once casually performed by the next-door neighbor. These days, however, lifestyles are such that the job is bigger than what most next-door neighbors can comfortably handle. A professional is needed to provide the kind of attention and care that pet owners are looking for today.

Petsitters perform a number of different functions, both for people who have gone away for short periods of time and for those whose hectic schedules don't permit them to spend as much time with their pets as they should. Vacationing families hire petsitters to feed the pets once or twice a day, walk the dog, pet the cat, and talk to the bird. Dog owners who work all day sometimes hire petsitters to come in and take the dog out for a stroll, keep him company, and even feed him his dinner if necessary.

DUTIES

The daily duties of a petsitter are a dog lover's dream come true. If you enjoy spending time with animals just for the sake of spending time with them, this is the job for you.

Petsitters who care for animals whose owners are away are responsible for determining if the pets are healthy, feeding them, cleaning up after them, playing with them, walking them (dogs only), and being in charge of their daily well-being. If a pet becomes sick, the petsitter takes him to the veterinarian; if the pet is ill, the petsitter medicates him. It is not unusual for petsitters to give injections to diabetic cats, take handicapped dogs for walks with their prosthetic devices attached, and even put drops in the eyes of pets with ophthalmic problems. All this is done in the animal's own home where the pet feels most comfortable. Petsitting is an alternative to boarding for people who prefer to keep their pets in a familiar environment and avoid the high costs of boarding more than one pet.

In addition to taking care of the animals in the home, most petsitters also water the plants, take in the mail, and monitor the security of the house.

Petsitters can also function as dog walkers and dog companions for people who don't want to leave their dogs home alone all day. It's the petsitter's job to go to the dog's home, take him out for a walk, play ball with him in the yard, and give him lots of tender-loving care.

WHAT IT TAKES

There are three important things you need in order to be a petsitter: a strong love and knowledge of different kinds of animals, a desire to work for yourself, and access to a car.

We know you love dogs—that's why you are reading this book. But because petsitting also calls for the care of cats, birds, hamsters, rabbits, and fish, you need to have a special place in your heart for all kinds of animals. If you love these animals but don't know much about their behavior and care, this is one area where you'll need to brush up.

The desire to work for yourself is important because petsitters are self-employed. Your petsitting operation will be a small business, run out of your home. You will be responsible for supplying the services rendered to your clients—you will also be the one in charge of keeping track of the bookkeeping and scheduling.

Unless you live in an urban area with excellent public transportation, you'll need access to a car. This is so you can drive from place to place as you care for your clients' pets. Most petsitters work within a limited geographical area to pare down the amount of driving they must do, but travel is an unavoidable part of the job.

Good health is another necessity for the job. Although most of the work involves feeding, walking, and cleaning up after dogs, there may be times when you have to lift a heavy pet. Make sure you can physically handle this kind of situation if it comes up.

Prospective petsitters need to be responsible and organized, since the care of many different animals depends solely on them. Because petsitters also have access to their client's homes and valuables, honesty and integrity are also mandatory.

ADVANTAGES

The most obvious advantage to being a petsitter is the opportunity to spend nearly all your working time taking care of animals—especially dogs. You will become a very important friend to the pets that need you in their owners' absence. They will learn to wait for your arrival each and every day and will greet you with great happiness and excitement. There are few things more rewarding than knowing you are bringing both physical and emotional comfort to a pet who has been temporarily separated from his family.

If you are like many working people, you'd prefer to answer only to yourself instead of to a superior. Petsitters have the advantage of being their own bosses, determining their own schedules, and making their own rules. Of course, you must do all this with your clients in mind, but it sure beats taking orders from a manager each and every day!

Another advantage of petsitting is that the more you work, the more you will get paid. For people who are used to working on a salary that doesn't change regardless of how many hours they put in, this pay-for-work situation is a real treat.

Petsitting is an easy business to start and maintain, with low overhead and relatively uncomplicated record keeping. Because it is a service industry, the primary commodity is you. Service-oriented companies can be among the best types of small businesses to run.

Since petsitters work out of their homes, they have the freedom to live anywhere they want. While you'll want to make sure you reside in an area with a rich client base, your work-at-home status enables you to put down roots in just about any area of the country that you would like.

DISADVANTAGES

Although being paid for the actual work you do can be a benefit, it can also be a disadvantage. Petsitters who are just starting out may find that business is pretty slow. You need time to build up your clientele and your reputation. While you are working on this, there won't be much income coming in.

Another disadvantage of being a petsitter is the traveling. You may spend a considerable amount of time getting from one client to another. This will require expenditures in the way of gasoline and car repairs, or money spent on fares if public transportation is your method of choice.

Petsitters have difficult schedules. While other people are off visiting friends and relatives on the weekends and on holidays, petsitters must stay close to home where their petsitting services will be needed.

Because petsitters are self-employed, they are obligated to pay for their own health insurance. They are also responsible for paying a self-employment tax, as well as Social Security and disability taxes.

EDUCATION

No formal education is required to be a petsitter. However, a strong background in animal care and some knowledge of business is vital if you are to be successful. Start by getting some experience taking care of pets. Volunteering at your local animal shelter can help you learn the ins and outs of animal care. You should also take at least one course in running a small business. Courses like these are offered through continuing education programs at local colleges and universities and are of minimal cost.

GETTING A JOB

When it comes to petsitting, getting a job means starting up your business. You can begin your new career by making up business cards, getting an answering machine if you don't have one already, and printing up flyers detailing your experience and your services.

You should also contact an insurance agent to begin the process of becoming bonded. If you are bonded, potential customers will be more likely to view you as honest and professional.

Your next step is to get the word out. Pay a visit to all the veterinary clinics, pet supply stores, and groomers in your area, and ask them if they will allow you to post your flyer on their bulletin boards. Give them your business card too, and ask them to refer clients in need of petsitting services to you. Be sure to dress and behave casually but professionally when you make these calls, since the impression you make will determine whether or not these establishments will send you their clients.

You may also want to use your doggy network to put the word out that you are offering petsitting services. Pay a visit to a dog show and talk to breeders. Give them one of your business cards and ask them to refer their puppy buyers to you. (Make sure to approach people at a dog show only *after* they have finished showing for the day.)

Consider running small advertisements in local dog show catalogs, daily newspaper classified sections and other inexpensive media that pet owners may utilize.

Once you get your business up and running, many of your clients will come from personal referrals. If you do a good job caring for someone's pets, chances are they will refer you to their friends.

SALARY

The salary for a petsitter depends largely on how much work the person does. Most petsitters charge anywhere from $10 to $15 per visit, depending on the number of animals, distance from the petsitter's home, and amount of work needed to be done. Successful petsitters in urban and suburban areas can make as much as $40,000 a year before taxes.

HUMANE WORK

For many people who love dogs, the tragedy of the animal over-population problem is a constant source of distress. The number of both dogs and cats that are destroyed every year because they have no homes is an outrage. The sight of a starving stray dog rummaging through a garbage can for a meal is heartbreaking. And hearing about the acts of cruelty still imposed on dogs in our supposedly civilized society is beyond disturbing.

If you are one of those animal lovers who wants to become actively involved in changing the harsh realities of animal over-population, abuse, and neglect, you may want to consider a career in humane work.

Animal-welfare advocates spend their days working in a variety of ways to educate and enlighten the general public on animal issues, while animal control officers roll up their sleeves and get out there to help the animals out on the streets. Both of these jobs can be rewarding if you have a deep personal belief in the humane treatment of animals.

POSITION: ANIMAL WELFARE ADVOCATE

 A few decades ago, the job of animal welfare advocate was nearly unheard of. With the exception of a few regional groups dedicated to the welfare of animals, there was no animal welfare community to speak of.

Now, things have changed dramatically. An increased awareness and concern for animals that started in the 1970s and grew over the past two decades has resulted in hundreds of national and regional organizations dedicated to improving the plight of pets everywhere.

The people who work at these mostly nonprofit organizations are animal welfare advocates. Functioning under a number of different job titles, these individuals are the heart and soul of the animal welfare movement.

There is a wide variety of positions held by animal welfare advocates. Many are involved in education, spending their time working to help teach the public how to better treat and care for animals in our society. Others are involved in fund-raising, constantly seeking out ways to finance a variety of animal assistance programs. Still others are involved in legislation, working to change the laws so they will provide adequate protection for domestic animals.

Whatever position you choose to pursue in the field of animal welfare advocate, you will find many rewards.

DUTIES

Because the positions held by animal welfare advocates are so varied, daily tasks are different from job to job. Educators spend much of their time devising and implementing programs that teach people about animal care and issues. Fund-raisers brainstorm to find new ways to appeal to the generous nature of many animal lovers. They strive to get the word out to these sympathetic citizens so they will continue to support animal programs and causes. Those in legislative positions, on the other hand, work with lobbyists to convince legislators to support proanimal bills and statutes.

Within each of these areas, there are different functions as well. Jobs in animal welfare organizations include positions in clerical support, management, and everything in between.

WHAT IT TAKES

The single most important quality in an animal welfare advocate is a profound dedication to the cause of animal welfare. This type of work can be extremely rewarding to those who care deeply about the well-being of animals, but for those who don't, the long hours and only moderate pay can be frustrating. If your personal sentiments lie with helping animals, you will find much satisfaction in a job as an animal welfare advocate.

Along with the rewards of helping animals, the disappointment of losing a battle on behalf of pets can be extremely frustrating and disillusioning. In order to be happy working as an animal welfare advocate, you have to be able to take the bad with the good and the losses with the wins. Despite the failures that animal welfare advocates regularly experience, you have to be able to maintain a positive attitude and stay focused on your ultimate goal of making the world a better place for pets.

ADVANTAGES

The greatest joy in being an animal welfare advocate is the knowledge that you are helping animals have a better quality of life. Animal welfare advocates have made huge advances in the lot of pets everywhere over the past few decades, and this is the ultimate reward for someone who truly cares about the well-being of animals. As you work each day to continue to foster the respect and concern that pets deserve in our society, you will feel the pride and satisfaction that only a career like this can bring.

Another great advantage to working as an animal welfare advocate is that you will be surrounded with people who are as passionate about the good of animals as you are. This provides the foundation of a strong support system, one that you will utilize on a daily basis as you fight the good fight for animals everywhere.

Unlike many other jobs with pets, the position of animal welfare advocate is an office position. This means you'll be working somewhat regular hours. In certain situations, you'll have to put in extra time during the week, and you may even have to work on a weekend or two. But generally speaking, the hours are similar to those of other office workers, leaving you with weekends and holidays to spend with your family and friends.

The benefit of a regular salary is another bonus of working as an animal welfare advocate. The uncertainties of being self-employed are not a problem for animal welfare advocates, especially those who work for large, well-established organizations.

DISADVANTAGES

There is one major disadvantage to being an animal welfare advocate, and that is the problem of ongoing frustration. For every battle that you win in the war to help animals, there will be at least one battle lost. It takes a special kind of person to live with this continuing disappointment and to focus on the victories instead of the losses. This is something many animal lovers find hard to do.

Although animal welfare advocates usually receive a regular salary, it is not one that is going to make them rich. Because most positions in this field are provided by nonprofit organizations dependent on charitable donations for their very existence, there is not a lot of money to go around. The exception can be for those advocates who rise to the top of their field and become presidents of some of the larger organizations. Several of these individuals make good salaries. However, compared to the presidents of privately run, for-profit companies, their salaries pale.

Another disadvantage of being an animal welfare advocate is the limited number of jobs that are out there. While this field has grown considerably in recent years, positions are still not available in every part of the country. In fact, the majority of jobs with the larger organizations are located in the Washington, D.C., area where proximity to the U.S. government allows these groups to more effectively lobby to change laws relating to animals.

EDUCATION

To obtain more than just a clerical support position at an animal welfare organization, you must have at least a four-year college degree under your belt. There is a wide variety of subjects you can choose from for your major depending on which area of animal advocacy you would like to work in. A major in liberal arts will qualify you in a general way, whereas a political science major can be helpful if you plan to go into the legislative arm of animal welfare. Those interested in education would do best getting a degree in a teaching-related field.

A resumé showing considerable volunteer work in the area of animal welfare will be very helpful when it comes to getting your foot in the door. Experience at an animal shelter will show employers that you have firsthand knowledge of the plight of pets in our society, and volunteer experience doing educational, fund-raising, or legislative work for a smaller organization will be equally impressive.

GETTING A JOB

Once you have completed your education and have performed some animal welfare-related volunteer work, you are ready to start job hunting. If you would like to stay in the same geographical area where you currently live, begin by applying to the animal welfare organizations nearby. Get the name of the person in charge of personnel or the individual who runs the department you'd like to work in, and send a cover letter and resumé. Follow up with a telephone call. Although there may not be a current opening, employers in this field will usually keep your information on file should a position come up. You should periodically follow up with a telephone call.

If you are willing to move to another area of the country to pursue your dream of being an animal welfare advocate, begin contacting organizations in the area you are interested in living, or send a cover letter and resumé to organizations throughout the country, if you have no geographical preferences.

It's also a good idea to join the organizations you are interested in working for, and learn about their policies and procedures. A membership will usually get you a subscription to the group's magazine or newsletter, in which you may learn about possible openings.

In addition, check the classified section of national dog magazines in the event that an opening may be advertised.

SALARY

The salary for an animal welfare advocate varies considerably, depending on the type of position, the geographical location of the organization, and the size and monetary health of the group. Entry-level positions can run anywhere from $15,000 to $20,000 per year. The presidents of some of the larger animal welfare organizations, individuals who are well-known and have been working in the field for many years, are close to the six-figure range.

POSITION: ANIMAL CONTROL OFFICER

 The day-to-day work of managing animal problems in our society is the job of the animal control officer, an individual who is responsible for the hands-on tasks required to maintain the health and safety of both animals and humans.

In the past, animal control officers were called "dogcatchers," and were not kindly thought of by animal lovers. Today, those sensitive to the problems of pet overpopulation understand that animal control officers are providing a needed service to unwanted and neglected animals who might starve to death on the street or die of painful injuries were it not for the animal control officer.

Animal control officers do more than help wayward animals. They also enforce public health codes, monitor public safety as it pertains to animals, and provide law enforcement services. They are employed by whatever local agency is responsible for the job of animal control.

DUTIES

Typically, animal control officers work out in the field, wearing uniforms and enforcing the humane laws of their local state and county. This can entail everything from gathering stray dogs and cats and having them impounded at the local animal shelter to investigating complaints regarding loose dogs, abused animals, and dog bites. Other animals also come under the jurisdiction of animal control officers, such as horses, snakes, and livestock.

Field officers are mobile and spend much of their time in agency-issued trucks. Their job entails handling a lot of animals, especially dogs. It also requires that they deal with the public on a daily basis. In some states, they are even licensed to carry firearms.

Animal control officers also work at shelters, functioning as kennel managers, animal care givers, and euthanasia technicians. This aspect of the job requires officers to work closely with pets that have been surrendered by their owners or picked up off the street by field officers. They are in charge of feeding the animals, providing them with supportive veterinary care, and cleaning up after them. Although there are some government-operated shelters that do not destroy unwanted pets, most do. At these shelters, euthanasia technicians are responsible for administering the injection that takes the lives of unwanted, unadoptable, or hopelessly ill cats and dogs.

WHAT IT TAKES

You have to be in good physical shape and have a strong emotional constitution to be an animal control officer, since much of the work in this field is difficult, both mentally and physically. You will see many disturbing sights as an animal control officer, and you have to be able to cope with this.

Animal control agents should not only like animals—they should like people too. Dealing with the public is a big part of the animal control officer's job. In fact, animal control officers find themselves having to employ whatever skills of diplomacy they might have, because they are often in tense and difficult situations. They also need some teaching skills, as part of their job is to educate pet owners on how to better care for their animals.

As both a pet lover and an animal control officer, you also need to be able to endure the dismaying sight of homeless and unwanted pets on a daily basis. The animal shelters you work with will be filled with these sad creatures, and in many cases, you will be the one bringing them there, knowing full well that the ones that don't find homes will be euthanized. If you function in the job of euthanasia technician, you will be the person who actually puts the animals down.

Because animal control officers are responsible for upholding the animal control laws in their area, they need to be the kind of people who respect the law and find satisfaction in enforcing it.

ADVANTAGES

There are a number of advantages to being an animal control officer. The first and foremost is the opportunity to help both people and animals. Bringing a starving and neglected dog to an animal shelter where it will be fed and cared for is a rewarding feeling. Even if the animal will be ultimately euthanized, the fact that you are helping to give it a humane and dignified death is comforting.

The opportunity to also help people is one of the benefits of being an animal control officer. Protecting the public from dangerous dogs and from health risks is an important and gratifying part of the job. For people who like to be active and outside instead of cooped up in an office building, animal control work can be a great job. Animal control officers are always on the go, traveling around their communities, and getting to know the people who live there and the animal issues that affect them.

Excitement is another perk that comes with the job. When you are out chasing animals and enforcing the law, there is no time to get bored.

And finally, when an animal you have saved from a bad situation finds a loving and caring home, it is a wonderful feeling. This is the kind of reward that comes often for animal control agents.

DISADVANTAGES

Stress is probably the single biggest disadvantage to being an animal control officer. People in this job suffer all kinds of verbal and physical abuse from the very public they are trying to protect. They also become depressed having to watch hundreds of animals being destroyed year after year in local animal shelters. This latter situation is especially hard for people who went into the field because they love dogs.

Animal control officers also endure the blame for a problem that is not their doing: animal overpopulation. While it is irresponsible pet owners that are the reason millions of animals are euthanized in shelters every year, animal control officers tend to get a bad rap because they are the ones who physically bring the animals to the shelter and humanely destroy them.

The job of animal control is physically and emotionally difficult, and there is often little support for animal control officers in the way of education, training, and counseling. Most animal control agencies are publicly funded and are short on money, ending up with officers who are overworked and underpaid.

Despite the difficulty of the job and the stress that comes with it, animal control officers are not well paid. In fact, it can be hard to survive alone on an animal control officer's salary. They also face the real possibility that they will be bitten by a frightened or aggressive animal they are trying to rescue.

EDUCATION

The minimum education for an animal control officer at an entry-level position is a high school diploma or GED. For those interested in moving into management, a four-year college degree is advantageous, preferably in business, science, sociology, or health. Formal on-the-job training is sometimes provided for animal control agents, in the areas of humane euthanasia, chemical capture, and other subjects relative to an animal control officer's work. The National Animal Control Association (see appendix) offers certification for animal control officers in these and other areas. The American Humane Association in Englewood, Colorado, also offers training for animal control workers.

GETTING A JOB

Prospective animal control officers can find work in a couple of ways. First, contact your local animal control agency directly by calling or sending a cover letter and resumé to the individual responsible for hiring. You can also check the employment section of your local Sunday newspaper for advertised positions.

SALARY

Most animal control officers start at the minimum wage or slightly above. Once on the job, specialized training can lead to salary increases. Those who go on to upper-level management and investigator positions can earn up to $85,000 a year in urban areas, $45,000 in mid-sized areas, and $24,000 in smaller communities.

HANDS-ON WORK

For many dog lovers, the jobs that offer the most physical contact with canines are the ones that are most appealing. When you can't get enough of being around man's best friend, hands-on careers like dog trainer, obedience instructor, groomer, and professional handler can be the absolute perfect positions.

Each one of these jobs, while offering daily contact with dogs, also requires certain character traits and specialized skills. Looking closely at each one will help you decide which job is best for you.

POSITION: DOG TRAINER

 Dog training is often viewed as one of the most glamorous positions in the world of canine careers. The idea of being able to communicate with a dog and have it do whatever you ask of it is an intriguing one, a notion that fascinates many people, dog lovers included.

Dog trainers can function in different capacities, depending on the area they choose to go into. They can work with pet dogs on behavior problems, helping these animals learn to live successfully in human society, or they can train service dogs for work with the handicapped and law enforcement. A few trainers even go into the entertainment industry, teaching dogs how to act in motion pictures and on television.

In this book, dog training differs in definition from obedience instructing. Here, dog trainers are those individuals who perform direct hands-on training of dogs. Obedience instructors concentrate on teaching both people and their dogs together.

DUTIES

The job of a dog trainer is pretty straightforward—you spend your time training dogs. Trainers who choose to go into business for themselves, offering their services to pet owners with problem dogs, will travel from one home to another, working with the dog. Some trainers prefer to work with the pet in their own facility and will maintain their own kennels to house their canine clients during schooling.

Trainers who teach police dogs and their handlers spend the day working with dogs and/or humans, educating them both so that they can work together. The situation is similar for trainers who teach bomb-sniffing dogs, assistance dogs for the handicapped, search and rescue canines, and working dogs for other capacities. The dog must be taught how to do its job, and the handler must be educated as well.

WHAT IT TAKES

In addition to a love of dogs, becoming a successful dog trainer requires a lot of patience and skill as a teacher. You will be spending many hours working with different dogs, usually of different breeds. Some will catch on quickly; others won't. You not only need to be patient with the ones that aren't as quick, but you also must be expert enough as a teacher to find ways to get through to the ones that need extra help.

A deep understanding of animal behavior—canine in particular—is mandatory if you are to be a good dog trainer. You have to know what a dog is thinking at just about any given moment, and you must be able to anticipate the same. Really good dog trainers have almost a sixth sense about dogs.

If you plan to be a dog trainer, you need to be the kind of person who enjoys working independently. Even those trainers employed by large training groups are on their own for a large part of the day. Except for the company of the dog you are training, you will be working pretty much by yourself.

Which is not to say trainers don't need good people skills. They do! Dog trainers need to be able to communicate with the pet owners they are working for, explaining the dog's problems, and coaching the owners on how to deal with the dog when the trainer is not there. This calls for a genuine concern for people. If you don't like people and think you can avoid having to deal with them completely by being a dog trainer, you are wrong.

ADVANTAGES

There are many advantages to being a dog trainer. The first is that you will get to spend much of your working hours dealing one-on-one with dogs. If you really love dogs, this is the greatest reward of the job.

Another advantage is that, as a dog trainer, you are in a position to work for yourself. Most dog trainers go into business for themselves, running their small service-oriented enterprises completely on their own. The overhead is low, and the ability to control just how much work you do is a real bonus. Some trainers work full time, while others only put in a few hours a day. The job holds a lot of flexibility.

As a dog trainer, your earning potential is high, especially if you own your own business. While most trainers make a moderate income, with time, experience, and reputation, you may be able to command fees that will put you in the upper tax brackets. There are some dog trainers who specialize in working with the pets of the rich and famous, and these trainers earn handsome livings.

The rewards of teaching a dog to be a better pet are tremendous. This is particularly true when you know you have saved the life of a dog that would have surely been put down because of its behavioral problems.

Trainers that teach assistance dogs for the handicapped, police dogs, and search and rescue dogs know that they are producing dogs that will help people as well. This provides a double bonus in terms of rewards.

Although the premiums are great, the time and money required to become a dog trainer are relatively small compared to other potentially high-paying jobs working with dogs.

And finally, dog training is just plain fun. You won't have much opportunity to get bored as a dog trainer. Every dog and every situation is different from the one before it, providing you with an endless variety of experiences.

DISADVANTAGES

There are only a few disadvantages to being a dog trainer. One is competition—there are a lot of dog trainers out there. Not all of them are good at what they do, so you will stand apart if you are especially talented. Getting your business started, however, and finding clients in an area already saturated with dog trainers can be difficult.

Dog trainers often have to deal with the results of someone

else's mistakes when it comes to dogs. Trying to teach a 100-pound dog to behave itself when it has spent the first year of its life running amuck with absolutely no discipline can be a real challenge. Trainers often have to deal with aggressive dogs who may even bite and sometimes recommend euthanasia for animals that can't be rehabilitated.

There are also the disadvantages that come with being self-employed, such as having to pay your own health care insurance premiums, and self-employment, Social Security, and disability taxes.

EDUCATION

While a talent for dog training may be inherent, you still need to formally learn the techniques behind this enjoyable profession. You can do this by studying with an experienced dog trainer or by enrolling in a school that specializes in teaching dog trainers.

If you want to learn from a trainer, you will need to spend some time (either paid or nonpaid) assisting a successful trainer. This could be an individual with her own business or a larger training group. You should tell your prospective employer at the time of your interview that you wish to learn to become a trainer yourself. If the individual or group agrees to mentor you, you can learn on the job.

However, most prospective dog trainers go to school to learn their trade. There are a multitude of dog training schools around the country whose exclusive purpose is to train people to become dog trainers. Some individuals even earn four-year college degrees in applied animal behavior before they embark on a dog-training career.

A high school diploma or GED is required to learn dog training only if you plan to attend a trade school or college. However, it is recommended no matter how you plan to acquire your skills, particularly if you plan to work for yourself. College-level business courses can also be a great asset, since most dog trainers are essentially small business owners and need to know the fundamentals of running their own company.

GETTING A JOB

If you plan to work for yourself as most dog trainers do, you will need a small amount of capital (under $1,000) to get your business set up. Advertising, promotion, and word-of-mouth are the most important ways you will get your clients. Give flyers and business cards to pet supply stores, groomers, and veterinary clinics, and ask them to recommend your services to their clients. Place ads in your local newspapers, and post flyers in every pet-related place you can find. You may even want to set up a booth at a local dog show or community fair so you can meet dog owners and tell them about your services.

SALARY

One of the best things about being a dog trainer is the potential salary. You will most likely start off at $8 to $10 an hour and will be able to charge more once your experience and reputation command a higher rate. Some trainers who own their own businesses make $60,000 to $70,000 a year. There are well-known trainers concentrating on high-profile clients who make even more than this.

POSITION: OBEDIENCE INSTRUCTOR

The job of the canine obedience instructor is different from that of the dog trainer, although their roles are similar. Whereas dog trainers spend most of their time training dogs, obedience instructors do most of their work with people.

Obedience instructors teach dog owners how to train and handle their own dogs. They usually do this in class settings, but sometimes work in situations where only one dog and its owner are present.

DUTIES

Obedience instructing consists of working with a class full of dogs and their owners, teaching the basics to the owners as they teach the same to their dogs. Instructors usually conduct several one-hour classes a day, with a schedule consisting of everything from puppy kindergarten classes to advanced obedience training. Instructors work with owners and dogs together as a group, and individually when needed.

Surprisingly, only about half of the instructor's time is actually spent in class. Filling out paperwork, getting class plans together, and talking on the telephone to clients, potential clients, and other business representatives make up the other half of the obedience instructor's day.

WHAT IT TAKES

Obedience instructors must know and understand dogs to be able to effectively help owners train them. They must have an empathy for dogs and be able to see things through the animal's eyes.

In addition to a love of dogs, obedience instructors must have a love of people as well. Most of the instructor's work is actually with people; the dogs are secondary. Because of this, obedience instructors must be able to deal with many different personality types.

Good communication skills are mandatory in the profession because obedience instructors must convey their knowledge of training to the owners in their class. In situations where individual owners are having difficulty understanding—or making their dogs understand—what is needed, the instructor must be able to explain and re-explain until the difficulty is resolved.

Problem-solving skills are essential to a good obedience

instructor, because dog training often poses many dilemmas that need to be worked out.

Obedience instructors also need patience, not only in class but also when it comes to building their business. It can take a long time to get the kind of recognition and popularity needed to run a successful obedience instructing business.

ADVANTAGES

There is a lot of satisfaction to be had in being a successful obedience instructor. Knowing you are helping dogs live happy lives with their families is a great reward. The knowledge that some of the dogs you work with may have ended up in an animal shelter, if not for your help, is very satisfying.

Because the profession of obedience instructor lends itself to self-employment, there is a lot of potential for freedom and flexibility in the job. You can determine your own teaching schedule and can even decide how many hours a day you want to work.

Successful obedience instructors reap the benefits of public recognition, if not nationally and internationally, then locally. People will admire you for your skills and respect you for the work you do. If you achieve great fame within the dog world—as a handful of obedience instructors have done—you may make a nice salary and have the opportunity to travel around the world.

DISADVANTAGES

When you first start out as an obedience instructor, it can be difficult to build your clientele. Considerable competition in the field, along with the fact that no one has yet heard of you, can make starting your business a challenge.

Once you do get your business up and running, you will find keeping it going to be a lot of work as well. In the profession of obedience instructing, there is little return business. Once a client's dog is trained, you don't usually hear from this person again until another dog arrives. Constant marketing and promotion is needed to keep the clients coming.

Frustration can be a big problem for obedience instructors, who can often find themselves dealing with people who just won't listen. After spending a considerable amount of time working with a dog and its owner, the owner may turn around and not follow the instructor's advice or, even worse, decide to follow the advice of a unknowledgeable friend or relative instead.

EDUCATION

Obedience instructors should have a high school diploma or GED, but this is not mandatory. Your training as an obedience instructor can begin at a community college or as part of a parks and recreation education program. Classes on dog training and obedience instruction are often provided through both of these sources.

You can also sign up for one of the many dog training schools that are devoted exclusively to teaching people how to train dogs, but this is not absolutely necessary to become an obedience instructor. You can teach yourself if you are motivated. Observe as many different obedience instructors at work as you can. Contact the National Association of Obedience Instructors or the Association of Pet Dog Trainers (see appendix) and ask for the names of members in your area. Contact some of these people and ask if you can watch their classes. It's important that you learn techniques from more than one person, since there are many different ways of training dogs and their owners.

It's also a good idea to work as an assistant obedience instructor. Here you can learn the ins and outs of teaching obedience classes with a mentor at hand. More than likely, you won't be paid for this work, but the experience you gain will be invaluable.

Another great place to get experience is at your local animal shelter. Get yourself a paid or volunteer position working with the dogs at the shelter, and stay there for one year. You can learn a tremendous amount in this environment.

While you are doing all this, don't forget to cultivate your people skills too. Taking classes or earning a matriculating degree in education can only help you be a better teacher, which is the essential role of the obedience instructor.

GETTING A JOB

If you plan to work as an independent obedience instructor in your own small business, you will need to set up shop somewhere and put the word out that your services are available. You may be able to lease space from a private building owner or make arrangements to use a local high school or other public building.

In order to get clients, you'll have to do some promotion and marketing. This means posting flyers, taking out ads in local newspapers and magazines, and talking to veterinarians, groomers, and pet supply retailers to let them know you are available.

If you don't want to go out on your own just yet, you can try getting a job at an obedience school or the obedience department of a large pet supply retail chain. This will provide you with a steady salary while you are gaining experience and learning more about the business. However, be aware that most of the large retail chains do not currently provide obedience instructors with continuing education, so this is something you will need to pursue on your own. This is important if you want to continue to grow and learn in your new profession.

If you are going out on your own, it will take some time to build your clientele. Have a considerable amount of money saved or another means of support during this period so you can survive.

SALARY

If you are successful at promoting your obedience training services, you can expect to earn anywhere from $25,000 to $30,000 annually in your first year.

If you decide to work for an obedience school or retail chain, your wage will be around $8 to $10 per hour.

POSITION: GROOMER

 If you have an intense passion for dogs plus artistic talent, you may want to consider becoming a dog groomer. Dog groomers are responsible for making dogs look good and for helping owners feel good *about* their dogs. They also take care of a dog's coat, keeping it healthy, clean, and free of the problems that arise when a dog is poorly groomed.

Groomers are often self-employed, working for themselves out of their homes or renting a space in a grooming shop. Some work for the grooming departments of large pet supply stores, and others are employed by veterinarians who want to offer grooming as a service to their clients.

DUTIES

The most obvious part of a dog groomer's job is making each and every dog look as beautiful as it possibly can. The details involved in this endeavor include brushing, bathing, blow drying, brushing some more, scissoring, and clipping. Ears are cleaned and toenails are trimmed.

On a dog that is groomed regularly, this is the routine. On dogs that are never groomed, or groomed very rarely, the work is a lot harder. It involves dematting, detangling, and a lot of elbow grease to get the coat back into the shape it's supposed to be.

The daily duties of a professional groomer also call for a lot of interaction with the public. You will need to talk to dog owners to not only find out what they want for their pet in the way of grooming but also to educate them in how to better care for their animal's skin and coat.

Cleaning up is also another job of the groomer. Brushed out hair and clipped toenails need to be swept up after a grooming session. Occasional bathroom accidents will also need to be handled by the groomer.

WHAT IT TAKES

You must have a great love and passion for dogs if you want to embark on a career as a professional dog groomer. You will be spending almost all your working time with your hands on one dog or another, striving to make that animal look its very best. Only someone who truly loves dogs can enjoy this type of work and do well at it.

Groomers are sculptors, in a way, using a dog's coat to create a work of art. To be good at grooming, you need to be an artist at heart, someone who likes to create beauty for the pleasure of others.

Patience is a virtue and an important part of being a groomer. Because you will be spending a lot of time working with pets who will not always be happy about what you are doing, you need to have lots and lots of patience. You will be handling more than one wet, struggling dog each and every day (and maybe even an occasional wet, struggling cat as well), and you have to have the kind of personality that won't allow this kind of behavior to drive you up a wall.

You also need good people skills. You will be coming face-to-face with pet owners on a daily basis, some of whom have never given their dogs a bath—ever. They will expect you to take their dirty, matted, flea-infested dog and turn it into something they saw while watching the Westminster Dog Show last February. You will need the skills of a diplomat and the forbearance of a clergyman to cope with these kinds of owners.

Prospective groomers also need to be in good health and have at least moderate physical strength in order to be able to do the job. You will spend almost your entire day on your feet, lifting dogs of various weights, and contorting your body in a number of ways as you bathe, scissor, clip, and brush. If you already have a bad back, forget about being a groomer. The day-to-day efforts of the job will have you in constant pain. If you have carpal tunnel syndrome, the chores of grooming will aggravate your problem. If you are allergic to dogs, you should choose another trade, since groomers are emersed in dander and hair for many hours a day.

ADVANTAGES

Being around dogs day in and day out is the greatest advantage of being a groomer. Your entire work world will revolve around making dogs feel good and look good. You'll get to interact with them, hang out with them, and become their friends. You will leave them feeling clean and well-cared for, and you will make their owners proud of them. This last aspect of the job is particularly rewarding.

Another advantage of being a groomer is the freedom it allows. If you choose to work for yourself, you will be in a position to make your own hours and work from home if you want to. There are even mobile groomers, people who set up grooming shops in a van and travel around to make grooming house calls on their customers. If you like the idea of being self-employed, grooming is a good career choice for you. If you prefer the stability of a regular paycheck, you can go this route too.

DISADVANTAGES

There are several disadvantages to being a groomer. One is the physical labor involved in the job. It can be tiring to stand up for most of the day, bent over a sink bathing a dog or twisted around trying to get out a particularly stubborn mat. Lifting dogs up and down from the table and sink can be tiring too.

The environment groomers work in, while fun because it is filled with dogs, can also be uncomfortable. Grooming shops tend to be hot, humid, and filled with flying dog hair and noisy blow dryers. Working under these conditions can be stressful.

Groomers can suffer from frustration brought on by neglectful or ignorant dog owners. A longhaired dog that has not been groomed for months is a nightmare to a professional groomer. Owners often expect the groomer to take an uncared for dog like this and turn it into something beautiful. In reality, the coat can be in such bad shape that the groomer's only option is to clip it down. Other times, groomers must spend hours trying to remove mats from a dog's coat, simply because the owner never bothers to brush the dog.

If a groomer is self-employed, he faces the usual perils that come with working for oneself. Expensive health insurance, self-employment tax, and an uncertain income are all the disadvantages of those who work for themselves.

And finally, there are the not-so-glamorous sides of grooming, such as the sweeping up of discarded hair, the cleaning up of bathroom accidents, and the expressing of anal glands, all tasks required of groomers. Groomers are also at risk of being bitten by dogs who don't appreciate the process of becoming beautiful.

EDUCATION

The professional groomer's education usually begins with one of the many grooming schools in North America, where a high school diploma or GED is usually required. Here, a prospective groomer can learn all the mechanics of grooming. Trade schools specializing in grooming programs will teach you how to bathe, clip, scissor, hand strip, and trim dogs of varying breeds, including mixed breeds. You will also learn how to handle dogs, as well as general canine care. Some schools even provide management training for those who are interested in running a grooming shop with several employees.

When choosing a trade school, make sure you select one that will teach you the skills you want to know when you become a professional groomer. Some schools offer financial aid and job placement assistance. If these are important factors for you, enroll in a school that will provide you with these benefits.

Once you graduate from grooming school, you will need to get on-the-job experience. Your certificate from the grooming school prepares you to start your grooming career, but real-life experience is vitally important. You may want to start out as an apprentice or assistant groomer, working with someone more experienced. Eventually, if you apply yourself, you will learn enough to go out on your own. If you prefer to start out right away as a groomer, work side-by-side with a more experienced groomer, one who has been in the profession for at least five years.

If you plan to own your own business, you may also want to take a course in running a small-business; such courses are usually offered as part of local college adult education programs. This will help prepare you for the task of managing your grooming business and will increase the likelihood of a profitable career.

GETTING A JOB

If you have wisely decided to work with another, more experienced groomer before going out on your own, you'll need to pound the pavement, handing out your resumé to various grooming shops and letting other professionals in the dog world know that you are looking for a job.

One of the more recent trends in the world of dog grooming has been the expansion of grooming departments in large pet supply chains. Many of these stores employ a number of groomers, and this can be a good place to start out.

Veterinarians with larger practices are also hiring groomers in order to provide an added service to their clients. Find out which veterinarians in your area employ groomers, and let them know you are looking for work.

Once you decide to become self-employed, getting a job means hanging a shingle out and going into business. Of course, there is much involved in this: finding a place to do your grooming (either your own shop or a leased spot in a grooming station), purchasing equipment, creating marketing and promotional materials, putting the word out about your services, and getting your services up and running.

SALARY

The salary range for professional groomers is usually $30,000 to $50,000. If you are self-employed, it may take you a while to earn this much since you will need time to build your business.

The owners of large grooming shops can make as much as $250,000. They have a number of other groomers working for them, and are able to service many clients.

POSITION: PROFESSIONAL HANDLER

 Of all the hands-on careers with dogs, the job of professional handler is probably the most glamorous. Professional handlers are those skilled individuals who take show dogs to the pinnacles of their career. Whether it be at a local breed specialty show or the Westminster event at Madison Square Garden every year, professional handlers are the ones often seen in the winner's circle smiling broadly with trophy and ribbons in hand.

There is more to being a professional handler than just those exciting moments in the show ring, however. Professional handling requires the ongoing care of client dogs, a strong commitment to the dogs in your charge, and an indepth knowledge of the dog world.

DUTIES

We've all seen the most visible part of the professional handler's job. The conformation class begins, and the handler brings the dog into the ring. She stacks the dog (makes it stand for the judge), gaits the dog (makes it trot around the ring), and keeps it always alert with a favorite toy or treat.

While it may look easy, there's a lot of preparation that goes into that glorious moment in the show ring. Many professional handlers do their own grooming, preparing the dog for its entry into the ring by bathing it, brushing it or hand stripping it, and clipping it, if necessary. Some of this is done the actual day of the show, not long before the class begins. Successful professional handlers have one or more assistants to help with much of this work.

Even more of the professional handler's work takes place long before the day of the show. Many of the dogs that are shown by professionals actually live with the handlers while they are being campaigned around the country. This means that the handler has the job of caring for these dogs day in and day out. This includes feeding and exercising the dogs and cleaning up after them. Most handlers have a kennel set up where the dogs are kept. Here, they are conditioned and primed for those special moments in the show ring.

Because professional handlers take their clients' dogs to shows around the country, traveling is a big part of the job. Most handlers bring several dogs to each show and usually drive to their destination in their own vans or RVs.

WHAT IT TAKES

A love for dogs and considerable knowledge about the various breeds is a requirement for anyone who wishes to be a professional handler. Since professionals work with a number of different breeds of dogs, they need to know how to groom, handle, and present each breed in the show ring. They also need to learn indepth the characteristics—both physical and mental—of each dog they are showing.

In addition to this, you need a flair for showmanship to be successful as a professional handler. You'll be out there in the show ring not just in front of a judge but also in front of a lot of spectators.

You must also be the kind of person who enjoys travel—or at least doesn't mind it. And you can't be a prima donna when it comes to doing the mundane work around the kennel—unless you are successful enough to be able to hire several assistants to do all the menial tasks.

Professional handlers also need to have good people skills. While much of your work is with dogs, you are also dealing with human clients. You will have their valuable and often well-loved show dogs in your possession for much of the year, and these owners need to be able to trust you. Your ability to communicate effectively with them will only help your business.

You also have to enjoy working independently to be happy as a professional handler. You and you alone are the one responsible for the success of your business, and you must be able to manage it and yourself wisely.

ADVANTAGES

Probably the biggest advantage to being a professional handler is the notoriety that comes as part of the job. Those handlers who are successful are well-known throughout the dog show world and are in high demand. Dog people will recognize you wherever you go, and they will be in awe of your handling skills.

Spending nearly all your time with dogs is another benefit to being a professional handler. In fact, if you play your cards right, the dogs you spend your time with will be some of the top show dogs in the nation!

If you make a big name for yourself as a professional handler, you can earn a very nice salary. You will also have the opportunity to see the country, and perhaps the world, if you cultivate the right clients.

DISADVANTAGES

Making a career as a professional handler is difficult. The competition in the show ring is stiff, and even with very good dogs, it can be hard to win time after time. Yet, this is the kind of performance owners look for in a professional handler. If you don't win on a very consistent basis, you won't have clients asking you to show their dogs.

With this reality comes pressure. Professional handlers are under a lot of pressure to win in the show ring, even if they don't have really great dogs to show. Once you make a name for yourself, this becomes easier because the dogs you are showing are of the highest quality. But you still need to beat the competition in the ring, and this is never easy.

If you are successful, the notoriety is great. Yet professional handling can be a lonely life at times. Handlers spend a great deal of time on the road away from their families.

Handlers are in charge of taking care of their clients' dogs, and are responsible for their well-being 24 hours a day. This means that you or someone else has to be looking after these dogs all the time, even while you are away at a show.

Although many people enjoy traveling, the constant journeying from one show to another can be exhausting. And unless you have your own RV or can afford the best hotels, your accommodations may not be too great either.

EDUCATION

There is no school to which you can go to learn to be a professional handler. This is something you must learn on your own through hands-on experience.

First of all, you need to start showing dogs, if you aren't doing it already. Enter your purebred dog in match shows and start practicing your handling skills. Once you know what you are doing, move up to classes at local specialty and all-breed dog shows. The key is to get as much experience as you can handling dogs in the ring. If you started handling dogs at a young age in junior show-manship, you are already ahead of the game.

Another way to gain experience in this field is to work as a handler's assistant. You will not only learn a lot about the dog show world this way, you may even have the opportunity to show some dogs yourself. While you are doing this, you need to be exhibiting your own dog on a regular basis, building up your handling skills and gaining recognition in the ring. You may offer to show your friends' dogs for free as well, because you'll need experience in handling more than one breed.

If you don't have a high school diploma already, it would be wise to get your GED. Then, take some business courses at your local community college. Being a professional handler means running your own small business, and you'll need certain skills to do it right.

GETTING A JOB

Once you know how to successfully take a dog into the show ring, it's time to start building a reputation. The best way to do this is to work with your own high-quality show dogs and to show them to some wins within the breed. People will notice you, and soon you will have your first clients. Spread the word within the canine community that you are embarking on a career as a professional handler, and the clients should start coming to you.

Another option is to work as a handler's assistant, gaining experience and attention in the show world by handling dogs for your employer. Eventually, you may want to go out on your own, finding your own clients to work for.

SALARY

If you start out as a handler's assistant, you will probably earn the minimum wage or slightly above.

Handlers usually charge clients by the class, in addition to a fee for boarding the dog while it is being campaigned. The amount you charge per class will be determined by your level of experience and success in the ring thus far. The boarding fees should be determined by your overhead, with some profit built in.

Handlers who are very successful in the show ring can make a very good salary, close to the six-figure mark.

CORPORATE PROFESSIONS

There is more to working with dogs than just dealing with them hands-on everyday. In fact, a whole, somewhat hidden world of corporate positions relating to dogs exists. While the veterinarians, groomers, and dog trainers receive most of the visibility, the corporate professionals in the dog world quietly work to make dogs' lives better.

Some of the more abundant of these positions include marketing specialists, editors, and attorneys. People who hold these jobs, while not directly involved with dogs each and every day, have a profound effect on the canine community.

POSITION: MARKETING SPECIALIST

 Have you ever wondered who is behind those amusing television advertisements for that certain dog food? Or who came up with the idea of pig ears as a dog treat? Marketing specialists—those people who are responsible for marketing and promoting products and services in the dog world—have a lot to do with these happenings and many others.

Marketing specialists do a lot of different jobs, among them product development, retailing, market research, and advertising and promotion. Although each of these positions is a distinct function, they all come under the heading of marketing. Large corporations and small one-person businesses all use the services of specialists in this field. In the case of big companies, there may be entire departments filled with individuals concentrating in one area. In a small business, one person may have all of these roles.

The pet supply industry is a huge business, employing thousands of people around the continent. Just like any other business, the skills of talented marketers are needed. Those individuals who not only know marketing but dogs too are invaluable.

DUTIES

The actual duties of each job within the marketing field vary considerably, but all require a knowledge of the business world and the dog world in particular. Those working in product development spend much of their time trying to come up with something new and exciting, whether it be a dog food or some revolutionary new toy. Retailers own and/or manage pet supply stores, selling their wares to the dog-owning public. For professionals involved in market research, conducting surveys and focus groups and studying dog-owner demographics are a large part of the job. In advertising and promotion positions, daily emphasis is placed on creating strategies to call attention to new and existing products.

WHAT IT TAKES

Marketers are special people in that they not only must have a strong understanding of business and economics, but they must also be creative. If you have both of these skills, marketing is an excellent career choice for you.

Unlike some of the other jobs in the canine world, a career in marketing requires a college education. You have to be the kind of person who likes school in order to successfully pursue the four- or six-year degree needed to get into the marketing field.

Although you love dogs, you have to be willing to deal with them in only a conceptual way while you are at work. It's rare that you will be working with real live dogs everyday unless you are involved in product development testing.

You must be cut out for office work, unless you choose to be a retailer. Nearly all marketing jobs are office jobs, and there's no way around it. You must also enjoy working on a team, because most marketing assignments are tackled as part of a group effort.

ADVANTAGES

There are some significant advantages to being a marketing specialist. The first is earning potential. Marketing specialists, depending on the area they choose and how high they rise into management, can make very good livings. In fact, the CEOs of large pet industry businesses often rise up through the marketing ranks.

Job security is another advantage. Marketing is a necessity in any business, and while marketers are subject to corporate downsizing just like people in other professions, no company can do without an adequately staffed marketing department.

One of the aspects of marketing that attracts people to it is the creativity factor. Marketing, whether you are working in advertising, retailing, or product development, calls for creativity. For most marketers, this is the best part of the job.

DISADVANTAGES

For people who love to be with dogs all day, a job in marketing can be a bit frustrating since you'll be spending nearly all your time just thinking and talking about dogs. Although an occasional canine will cross your workday path, most of your time will be spent contemplating man's best friend—not petting him.

Your first job in marketing will undoubtedly be with a company not in the pet industry. Companies in the dog business are scattered around the country, and there may not be any opportunities at the one in your home town. You will most likely have to slowly work your way toward a job in canine marketing and may even have to relocate to get it.

Marketing requires a four- or six-year degree and the time and money that goes along with pursuing a higher education.

EDUCATION

It is almost impossible to get a good corporate job in marketing with anything less than a four-year bachelor's degree. Candidates with master's degrees stand an even greater chance of getting hired. (Those individuals wanting to work as self-employed retailers are an exception to this rule.)

Some colleges and universities offer degrees in marketing. Others have majors that are acceptable for marketing careers. Many liberal arts majors go into marketing, as do business majors, communication majors, and journalism majors.

While you are attending school, take advantage of any marketing internships that are available. Paid or college-credit work in the field will help you later to get the job that you want.

In the process of getting your formal education, try to get as much experience in the dog world as you can. Volunteer at your local animal shelter. Offer to do promotional work for a breed club in your area. Get some dog-related marketing experience on your resumé for the day you go on your first marketing job interview in the pet industry.

GETTING A JOB

Before you start looking for a job, the first thing you need to do is realize that it's unlikely your first or even second marketing job will be in the pet industry. Although you should certainly make every effort to get a job in the canine-marketing field, there may not be a position available in the area where you live. Because entry-level marketing jobs don't usually pay well enough to warrant a relocation, your best bet is to get your foot in the marketing door at a company in the area where you live, and work toward getting the exact job you want as you progress somewhat in your career.

Eventually, once you have some marketing experience under your belt, start approaching some of the larger to mid-sized pet food and supply companies by sending out resumés and cover letters and calling to follow up.

SALARY

Marketing specialists can start out with an annual salary of anywhere from $20,000 to $27,000, depending on the area of the country, the company, and the job. There is potential to eventually earn a six-figure salary.

POSITION: EDITOR

Have you ever read through a dog magazine, amazed at how much information is included in its many pages? Does the world of publishing seem exciting to you? If so, take a close look at the job of dog editor.

Most of the jobs for editors specializing in canine subjects are in the magazine world. There are currently four major national, general interest dog magazines in the United States and Canada (*Dog Fancy*, *Dog World*, *AKC Gazette*, and *Dogs in Canada*). There are scores of smaller publications as well, from breed-specific periodicals and pet industry trade journals to regional monthlies. Monthly newsletters are also becoming more popular in the dog world. Several canine newspapers also exist and are published on a weekly basis. These papers tend to focus primarily on the dog show world, whereas dog-related magazines run the gamut from general care to conformation showing. There are also general interest pet magazines that cover not only dogs but cats, horses, and other companion animals as well.

Editors are the people who put these publications together, using a combination of journalistic skills and dog knowledge to create printed information of value for their readers.

DUTIES

The job of the editor includes many different duties. Although it varies from publisher to publisher, most editors are responsible for hiring writers to create the text and photographers to take the pictures. They are in charge of editing the copy, selecting the photographs, and working with a graphic designer to create the pages you see in print.

Editors also spend considerable time corresponding with authors and readers, attending dog-related events, and keeping abreast of happenings in the dog world. Some editors also write and take photos for the publication they edit.

The duties at the entry-level position vary from publication to publication, but most editorial applicants start out in the field by filing, answering phones, and doing only minor editing.

WHAT IT TAKES

To be happy working as an editor, you should be a detail-oriented person, one who enjoys working on a project from start to finish. Because editors often wear many hats, you also have to be flexible and able to juggle different assignments.

A respect for deadlines is essential if you want to be an editor, since deadlines are a part of an editor's daily life. If you get stressed out by the thought of having to meet several of these deadlines every month, you will not enjoy working as an editor.

Talent in and enjoyment of writing is another prerequisite for editors. Many publications are too small to hire freelance writers and often rely on the writing skills of staff editors to provide copy.

A love of the written word is mandatory if you want to be an editor. You'll be spending your time proofreading, copyediting, and correcting the English language, and only someone who loves language will enjoy this type of work.

ADVANTAGES

The best thing about being a dog publication editor is the subject matter. It's fun and exciting to think and talk about dogs all day long and to create a publication that is all about your favorite subject.

The editors of most dog-related publications have the added bonus of knowing that their work is helping to improve the lives of dogs everywhere. Articles about health, behavior, and general dog care help owners take better care of their pets, making life better for dogs.

It is very satisfying to see the finished product of your labor in printed form. When that magazine, newspaper, or newsletter comes back from the printer with your name in the masthead, you'll feel like you've really accomplished something.

The job of dog editor also comes with notoriety. Dog owners will come to recognize your name, and breeders, handlers, and others in the dog world will want to meet you and shake your hand.

DISADVANTAGES

One of the biggest problems for dog editors is salary. Compared to the salaries of other corporate professionals, editors are paid rather low. This is true of the publishing world in general but is especially true in the dog publishing world. Even a top position does not reap the kinds of financial rewards one might expect.

Staffs are often small on canine publications, which means the editors employed on each periodical are frequently overworked. It's hard to find a dog publication editor who works nine to five, five days a week. Long days and work-filled weekends are not uncommon in the editor's life.

Jobs in this field are not easy to come by. Many canine publications have very small budgets and can't afford to hire a lot of editors. The bigger publications are scattered around the country, and unless you are very lucky, you will probably have to relocate if you want to work on one.

No matter how hard you try, there will always be someone who is unhappy or offended by something you have published. There are many controversies in the dog world, and it's impossible for the editors of canine publications to avoid getting caught up in them. You'll get hate mail from the people who disagree with your publication's viewpoint and a nasty phone call now and then.

EDUCATION

In order to have a career as a dog editor, you need to earn at least a bachelor's degree. A master's degree is even better. Publishers of animal-oriented books and periodicals want to see a major in journalism or English, with a minor in a life science, preferably an animal-related one.

Pursue any internship opportunity that may come up in college. An internship at any publication can do wonders for your resumé. If no internships are available, volunteer to work on your school paper.

Your dog background is important too. While you are going to school, get as much experience as you can working with dogs, whether it's volunteering at an animal shelter or working as a veterinary assistant. You may even want to volunteer to edit the newsletter or newspaper of a local dog club. Study dogs on your own, learning as much as you can about the different breeds and the way dog shows work. Knowing the lingo of the dog world is a great asset when working as a canine editor.

GETTING A JOB

It's unlikely that your first job in publishing will be dog-related since these jobs are hard to come by—and publishers in the field are scattered around the country. Start out in your career by working on another publication. The field of publishing is rather specialized, so get started in the type of publication where you ultimately want to end up. If you want to be a magazine editor on a consumer magazine, get a job on a consumer magazine. If you want to edit a newspaper, make your first position a newspaper position.

When you go searching for that first job, if you can't find a job on a dog publication, try to find one on a periodical with an animal-related subject matter. Horses, cats, and other companion animals are the best, but if that's not possible, a livestock publication will suffice. If there's nothing like this in your area, try a medical publication or one that focuses on the natural sciences. With a background like this, you are more likely to attract a canine publisher's eye somewhere down the road.

The placement office of your college or university can help you get your foot in the door of that first publication.

Once you've had a few years' experience as an editor, you can start sending your resume and cover letter to the various dog publications around the country. Follow up with a phone call. Let them know that your dream is to work on a dog publication and that you are eager to relocate to their area. Although there may not be an opening at the time you contact them, be patient and persistent. If you keep trying, the right job will eventually come your way.

SALARY

Magazine editors usually start out at around $20,000 per year, newspaper staffers slightly less. Newsletter editors may make more than this, depending on the type of company they work for. There is potential to earn several times this amount if an individual rises to the top of the field.

POSITION: ATTORNEY

 Why in the world would a dog need an attorney, you may wonder. Actually, dogs and their owners manage to regularly get into a number of situations that require legal assistance. Attorneys who love dogs are in the position to help these individuals by specializing in canine legal cases.

It's unusual to find an attorney who works only on dog-related actions, but there are several individuals in the field who seek out projects specifically related to dogs. These attorneys litigate in dog bite cases, cruelty matters, and in other canine-related situations.

DUTIES

There are many different types of lawyers, and the duties of each depend on what type of law they are practicing. Litigation attorneys spend much of their time in court, representing their clients before a judge and sometimes a jury. They also devote much of their time meeting with clients. Research lawyers investigate cases to aid litigation attorneys in court. Transactional attorneys handle contracts and other legal paperwork.

WHAT IT TAKES

Each different area of law calls for certain personality traits.

Litigation attorneys have to be quick on their feet in order to handle courtroom situations. They must also be persuasive and likeable. Research and transactional attorneys must enjoy reading, writing, and analyzing, because this is what they spend most of their time doing.

No matter what type of law you decide to practice, you must be the kind of person who enjoys hard work. Being a lawyer is difficult and requires many hours on the job.

In order to understand and work with the intricacies of the law, you must be a person of considerable intelligence. You must also like school, since earning a law degree requires additional schooling beyond the four-year degree.

People skills are a must for attorneys, because they find themselves dealing with many different personalities on a daily basis. You must know how to communicate effectively with your clients and provide them with the feeling that they can trust you with their legal problems.

Finally, you must have a genuine love and fascination for the law. Without this trait, you won't be happy working as an attorney.

ADVANTAGES

If you are able to include dog-related cases in your legal practice, the advantages to the job are many. You can take on cases that will help both dogs and people, and you'll be immersed in a subject that you love.

Prestige is another reward in being an attorney. While some people dislike lawyers, most people are in awe of their skills and knowledge. You'll be considered a valuable member of the community, especially if your work is geared toward helping dogs and their owners.

If you are a competitive person, you will love being an attorney. The thrill of winning a case is one of the great joys of the job. The challenge of working to succeed in each legal situation can be rewarding as well, regardless of the ultimate outcome.

As an attorney, you will also reap the rewards of a comfortable salary, usually determined by how many hours you put in at the job.

DISADVANTAGES

Stress is probably the biggest drawback to being an attorney. Lawyers work long hours under considerable pressure from their bosses and/or clients. There is frustration when you lose a case or fail to achieve a goal for your client, and these losses can ultimately hurt your career.

If you want to practice dog law only, you will have a hard time making ends meet. Most attorneys specializing in canine cases also do other kinds of legal work as well in order to subsidize their business.

The time and cost of going to law school is significant. It's hard work, and many graduates are left with considerable debt to pay back.

Most attorneys work long hours, and this includes many weekends and even holidays.

Believe it or not, attorneys don't make as much money as you might think. In fact, for the amount of schooling required and time put in at the job, their salaries are relatively low. The exception to this rule are the high-profile plaintiff attorneys that have become household names and some lesser-known corporate attorneys. These individuals make exorbitant amounts of money. However, the majority of lawyers do not earn these kinds of salaries.

EDUCATION

In order to become an attorney, you must graduate from an accredited law school and pass a bar exam proving that you know enough to practice law. In some states, you will also be required to pass a professional responsibility exam as well.

Before you can enter law school, you need to be a high school graduate with a four-year degree. (Some law schools do not require a four-year degree, but will confer a four-year undergraduate degree on you after you have completed the necessary units.) Good prelaw college majors include political science and English. Whatever major you decide to pursue, make sure you take a lot of writing and speech classes, since much of an attorney's job involves both written and oral communication. Your college grade point average should be high, because this will be weighed heavily by the admissions personnel of the school to which you are applying.

To be accepted into law school, you also need to pass a Law School Admissions Test (LSAT). Potential law schools will not only look at your college GPA, but will also take your LSAT score into consideration.

Make sure you do some work in the community as well to increase your chances of being accepted into law school. This can include dog-related activities, but because law schools look for individuals with well-rounded backgrounds, your experience should also consist of work in other areas as well.

While you are attending law school, take advantage of your school's legal clinics. Here, students are given the opportunity to do pro bono work to benefit the community while at the same time gaining legal experience. Try to write for your school's law review as well. While a position on the law review can be time-consuming and difficult to obtain (high grades are required and there's a lot of competition), it will be an excellent addition to your resumé.

While you are attending law school, you may also want to get a job working as a law clerk in a legal office, district attorney's office, or pro bono clinic, or take a summer position as a judge clerkship. Any of these positions will give you needed experience, as well as something beneficial for your resumé.

GETTING A JOB

If you want to become an attorney who specializes in canine cases, your best bet is to go out on your own into a private practice. Before you do this, you might want to work for a partnership or corporation in the field of law you are pursuing. This way, you can get some experience under your belt before you go out on your own.

Once you are ready to start building your canine law career, begin by seeking out dog-related cases. Network with dog people at shows and other events, and spread the word that you specialize in canine law. You may even want to advertise your services in dog magazines and other canine publications, but do this in a tasteful way. Once you get a few clients and are successful at helping them, word of mouth will help you find even more.

Remember that even though you would prefer to work only dog-related cases, you will probably need to take on other projects as well. Don't neglect this other part of your practice while you are seeking out canine clients.

SALARY

The salary range for attorneys varies quite considerably, depending on the type of law they wish to practice and who they are working with. If you start out working for a legal firm or corporation, you will earn at least a minimum salary in the mid to high 20s. Eventually, you can earn two or three times that, depending on the employer and the type of work you do.

Attorneys in solo practice can earn a lot or a little, depending on how many hours they put in and what type of law they practice.

CREATIVE POSITIONS

Although nearly every profession relating to dogs requires some creativity, there are certain jobs that rely quite heavily on creative talents.

Those who earn their livings as commercial artists, commercial photographers, and freelance writers spend much of their time immersed in the creative process. Dogs happen to make excellent subjects in each of these three inventive positions and often provide great inspiration to the creative mind.

It's true that people who love dogs generally enjoy artistic representations of their favorite animal. Whether it be a painting, a photograph, or a piece of writing, if it's good, dog lovers want to possess it, be a part of it, and make it their very own.

POSITION: COMMERCIAL ARTIST

 People who love both art and dogs often dream of making a living by combining both of these passions. If the thought of spending nearly all of your working time painting or sketching the likenesses of dogs sounds like a dream come true to you, you may want to consider becoming an artist who specializes in canine subjects.

There are a number of markets for dog art, including individual dog owners who will commission you to paint or sculpt their pet; publishers who will hire you to illustrate books or magazine articles; corporations who will contract you to create designs for products; and dog lovers who will buy your art simply because they like it. You can use one or more of these markets to make a living with your artistic talents.

DUTIES

Most artists who paint, sketch, or sculpt dogs are self-employed, working on their own in whichever medium they have chosen. They are, in essence, small business owners, selling both a service and a product.

Those artists that work on commission for dog owners usually create from a photograph of the pet and will oftentimes visit the dog in person to become well acquainted with the dog's physical appearance and personality. Once the artist knows the animal well, he will go back to the studio and work for days, weeks, or even months to create the perfect canine portrait.

Artists who work for publishers and corporate clients are usually hired to illustrate a specific to-be-published work or product. The client will provide the artist with the raw text of the book or article or with information on the marketing concepts that the artist is to follow when creating the contracted work. If the artist works in different mediums, the client will often request that the work be done in the one most appropriate to the job.

Artists also have the option of more directly selling their original artwork or prints to the public. This type of work entails creating pieces that the artist believes will have commercial market value and advertising them to dog lovers. This can be done through a retailer or catalog company or handled directly by the artist.

WHAT IT TAKES

In order to make it as an artist, you must have a great passion for your work. You must love to spend time in a studio alone, creating in the medium or media you have chosen, since this is what you'll be doing most of your day.

You also need to be the kind of person who doesn't give up easily. It's difficult to find success in this very competitive field, and perseverance and persistence are necessary if you are going to make it.

Talent is another very important necessity to success as an artist. Unfortunately, desire and drive to be an artist do not always go hand in hand with actual ability. Although you can learn a lot about art through a formal education, actual talent must be inborn.

Even though you are a creative person, you can never lose sight of the fact that people are paying you for your work. You must be able to distance yourself enough from your artwork so you can take criticism from clients who may not always like what you produce the first time around. Don't allow yourself to become the stereotypical temperamental artist. Remember that you are a business person, as well as a creative person, and your livelihood depends on pleasing your audience.

Flexibility is important in the field of commercial art. You must be willing to create works on other subjects, as well as dogs, in order to survive. There may not be enough dog-specific work in your geographical area to sustain you, and branching out to include other animals, even people or a variety of other subjects, can help you succeed in your business.

And finally, you really need to know dogs. The anatomy of different breeds must be a part of your knowledge bank, along with a feeling for canine behavior and temperament.

ADVANTAGES

The greatest advantage to being a canine artist is the realization of a dream. If you have been driven to paint, sketch, or sculpt dogs for a very long time and then suddenly find yourself successfully doing this for a living, the personal rewards and satisfaction are immense.

Most artists are self-employed, which means that they are their own bosses. Although you must take some direction from your clients, you are pretty much free to create whatever and however you want. Like most self-employed people, you also have the freedom to set your own hours and come and go as you please.

If you become well-known in the canine art field, you will enjoy an amount of public recognition rarely experienced by most canine professionals. Knowing that many other dog lovers truly value and appreciate your work can be extremely gratifying.

DISADVANTAGES

The biggest disadvantage to being an artist is the inherent difficulty in trying to "make it." There is a lot of competition out there, and it can take years before even a very talented artist receives the recognition she deserves. It could be a long time before you are able to earn a living as an artist, and you may find yourself having to work doing something else just to pay the bills.

Unless you are wildly successful, there isn't a lot of money in it. Canine artists enjoying even moderate success earn rather small incomes. You would have to be the canine equivalent to Salvador Dali in order to get rich painting dogs.

Producing artwork requires a great deal of creativity, and for commercial artists, that creativity must be readily available on a moment's notice. Unlike those who produce art as a hobby, commercial artists must find a way to be creative even when they aren't in the mood.

Being an artist can be lonely much of the time. You will spend long hours alone in your studio with your work. For people who crave human companionship on a daily basis, this isolation can be difficult to take.

Along with other self-employed professionals, artists who work for themselves must pay for their own health benefits and retirement and contribute Social Security and self-employment taxes to the government.

EDUCATION

There are a number of different ways to become a commercial artist. If you are the academic type, you can pursue a four-year college degree in art where you will not only learn about the mechanics of creating artwork but also the history behind it. Many artists find this type of education invaluable, because it helps them develop their own unique style and philosophy.

Another option is to attend a trade school or take individual classes in art from a local college. Fundamentals like anatomy and color will be taught here, giving you the foundation you'll need to become good at what you do.

There are some artists who do not engage in any formal schooling and instead, teach themselves how to paint, sketch, or sculpt. You can go this route if you prefer, but be aware that some type of art education, no matter how small, can be of great benefit in the future.

Because artists are also small-business owners, a class or two in small-business management can also prove very helpful.

GETTING A JOB

Once you go out on your own, you will need to market yourself in the area you have chosen to concentrate in. If you want to do commissioned portraits, you must let the dog-owning public know about your services. Use your network of dog professionals to get the word out. Tell everyone you know about your services, and hand out business cards whenever you can. Hang flyers up at the pet supply stores and veterinary offices in your area. Place advertisements in dog magazines and all-breed club newsletters—anywhere that dog owners might see them. Include a photograph of one of your canine portraits so people can see what your work looks like. Make sure you create a realistic advertising budget for yourself, and place your ads in the publications that are most likely to reach the readers that you want.

If you are pursuing publishers and corporate clients, put together a portfolio of your work, and submit copies to the companies you would like to work for. Find out exactly who is responsible for hiring artists at the company, and follow up with a phone call a couple of weeks after sending in the samples of your work. It can be hard to break into a publisher or corporation, but if your work is very good, it will stand out among all the other submissions. Eventually, you will get some work, and this will lead to even more.

If you prefer to market your artwork directly to the public, either through a retailer or catalog, you'll have to put on your salesperson hat and start beating the pavement. Contact retailers and catalogers who sell canine products and/or artwork, and show them your work. Your job is to convince them that your art will help them make money and deserves a valuable place on their shelf or catalog page.

If you want to try selling directly to the public, you'll need to get out there and market your artwork yourself. Booths at craft fairs, street fairs and dog-related events like shows and performance events are good ways to present your artwork to the dog-loving public. You can also try advertising in dog magazines, newsletters, and other publications geared toward dog owners.

SALARY

When you first start out as an independent commercial canine artist, you will make very little money, possibly nothing at all. It may take a good five to ten years to build up enough of a clientele to make an even moderate living of $25,000 a year.

Some artists specializing in dogs who have reached considerable fame earn six-figure salaries. However, these individuals are most definitely the exception and not the rule.

POSITION: COMMERCIAL PHOTOGRAPHER

We've all taken pictures of our dogs just for the fun of it. But if you are *very* into photography and see the dog as your number one subject, consider a career as a commercial canine photographer.

There are a number of markets for commercial photography involving dogs. Among them are portrait photography, stock photography, and dog-show photography. Many dog photographers sell their work in more than one of these markets, finding the profession to be both exciting and rewarding.

DUTIES

The day-to-day duties of a canine photographer vary depending on the type of market she has chosen to pursue. Portrait photographers who shoot on the owner's property spend a lot of time traveling from client to client. Both traveling photographers and those with their own studios spend time setting up lights, backgrounds, and camera equipment. Once the dog is photographed, the photographer either does the film developing or takes it to a lab to be processed. Pet owners display these photographs in their home or send them to friends, and breeders use them to advertise their dogs.

Stock photographers spend a lot of time going from place to

place taking candid pictures of dogs that will ultimately be published in books and magazines. The dogs they shoot can be at breeders' homes, at dog shows, in the fields, or assisting the handicapped. Sometimes these photographs are purchased by stock agencies, which in turn sell them to publishers. In other situations, the publishers themselves hire the photographers to take pictures for a specific book or article.

Dog show photographers travel from show to show taking the official pictures of the winners of each class. Owners can then purchase copies of these photos for their own use. Canine magazines and periodicals sometimes purchase the rights to use these images in conjunction with articles they are publishing.

WHAT IT TAKES

In order to be successful as a commercial photographer specializing in canine subjects, you must have a real passion for photography. Like other professionals in creative careers, photographers who are just starting out face a great challenge. It can be a difficult road ahead, and you need real motivation to persevere.

Assertiveness is another valuable trait in a commercial photographer. Although there's a big difference between a member of the *paparazzi* and a canine photographer, even photographers who take pictures of dogs need to get out there and get the best shots. This is especially true of professionals specializing in candid photos.

Photographers need to get the best out of their subjects when taking pictures. Since your subject will be dogs, you need to have knowledge of their behavior and the ability to handle whatever canine antics you may encounter. In the case of portrait photography, nervous dogs need to be soothed, and "couch potatoes" need encouragement just to look alert. Dealing with canine personalities is a big part of the dog photographer's job.

Talent and technical skill are also very important in the field of commercial photography. You need to have a good eye and a real gift for composition. You must also have the technical know-how required to produce a great photograph, one with just the right lighting, depth of field, and use of color.

However, talent and skill alone are not enough—you also need some capital to buy all that equipment you'll need to get your business started. Because commercial photographers essentially run their own businesses, you will need a bit of business savvy to know how to handle the details of managing your small company.

Finally, people skills are of great value to the commercial photographer. You'll be dealing with a lot of humans, as well as dogs, in this field, and the ability to be diplomatic, communicative, and easy going will help you in your career.

ADVANTAGES

Being a commercial dog photographer can be a lot of fun. You will be working closely with dogs, day in and day out, taking their pictures and capturing their most endearing and exciting moments. If you love dogs, this part of the job will provide you with real joy.

The creativity involved in making great photos is one of the joys of working in this profession. Photographers are artists, creating visual imagery that can be both beautiful and emotionally stirring.

Being a photographer is a somewhat glamorous job. At dog shows and other events, people will want your attention. Handlers will be stacking their dogs for you left and right, and owners will be clamoring for you to take a shot of their special pet.

Depending on the kind of photography you do, there may be opportunity for travel. Dog show photographers, in particular, are in a position to travel all around the country, taking pictures of the top dogs in the land while also getting a glimpse of how people—and their dogs—live.

Because you will be self-employed, you will have the freedom of setting your own hours, working as much or as little as you want, and coming and going as you please. This is one of the most appealing aspects of commercial photography and self-employment for a lot of people.

DISADVANTAGES

Although canine photography is both fun and exciting, it is also very difficult to break into. There is a lot of competition out there, and a photographer may have to pursue this field for a long time before finding career success.

When success does come, it's not as lucrative as you might think. Good commercial dog photographers with a lot of clients can make a fairly decent living, but this is not the kind of career that will get you rich. In fact, many dog photographers also take pictures of other kinds of animals or even people to help subsidize their business.

The start-up costs for a commercial photographer can be high. A studio, lighting and camera equipment, a darkroom—buying all these items can easily run you into the thousands, with no guarantee of work once the purchase is made.

EDUCATION

Commercial photographers are sometimes self-taught, but most attend either a four-year college to get a degree in photography or go to a trade school for training. Because technical know-how is important in this field, it's a good idea to get at least some kind of formal training.

While you are learning about photography, you should also be building up your skills with dogs. Spend time handling them and even taking their pictures just for the fun of it. You will learn the peculiarities of photographing canines, something that won't be covered much in your formal education.

Be sure to take some classes in running a small business too, because as a self-employed photographer, you'll be in charge of the daily machinations of your own small company.

GETTING A JOB

Because you'll be working on your own as a commercial canine photographer, you'll need to decide what type of market you plan to pursue, get your equipment together, and start promoting your services.

For portrait photography, you'll need to get your name out to dog owners and breeders. Advertise in local dog club publications, and put up flyers at veterinarians' offices and pet supply stores. Set up a booth at dog shows in your area to display your work.

If you wish to get into stock photography, you'll need to build up a library of various canine photographs. Once you've done this, research some of the stock photo houses that purchase animal photographs, and speak to them about buying your work. You can also contact dog magazines directly, either by submitting some samples of your work or asking them for photographer's guidelines.

Dog show photography is even more difficult to break into, since most show-giving entities are already working with established photographers. Use your professional canine network to get the word out that you are specializing in dog show photography, and you might get lucky. Be sure your message finds its way to the person responsible for hiring a show photographer for a particular event because he might be interested in trying you out.

SALARY

Canine photographers who are just starting out should expect some lean times. Don't be surprised if you don't make enough in your first year to even pay for the equipment you purchased. Do something else to bring in money while you build up your photography business. Eventually, if you are good at what you do and have perseverance, you may earn up to $55,000 or more as a commercial photographer.

POSITION: FREELANCE WRITER

 The information explosion is here, and now more than ever, there are scores of magazines, newspapers, books, and Web sites devoted strictly to the subject of dogs. Publishers have come to realize that people feel strongly about their canine companions and want to gain as much knowledge as possible in how to best care for and treat their pets.

This is where professional writers come in. Those who work with words as they relate to the subject of dogs create articles, columns, brochures, and books. They are responsible for helping to educate dog owners and making the world a better place for dogs.

Most professional writers who write about dogs are freelancers, self-employed individuals who work from home with little more than a telephone, personal computer, and answering machine. Their primary tool is their brain, which they use to research, interpret, and ultimately convey in words a multitude of information about dogs.

DUTIES

The job of the professional writer can be divided into two parts: research and writing. Depending on the type of material the writer is creating, the research can be broad, encompassing many different sources or, in the case of a breeder profile or coverage of a particular show, be limited to just a few sources. This research usually requires considerable telephone work and sometimes actual in-person interviewing. Occasionally, the library or the Internet come in handy when trying to pull together all the information one needs to write an article or a book.

The writing aspect of the job is both technical and creative. The writer takes the research information that was gathered and puts it into coherent form. In the process, she tries to make it as interesting and entertaining as possible.

Aside from the actual work of researching and writing a book or an article, freelance writers must also market their services. This involves writing query letters, contacting editors, and networking with fellow writers.

WHAT IT TAKES

Depending on your innate skills and abilities, writing can either be fun or very difficult. In order to enjoy your life as a freelance writer, you must love writing and find that it comes easily to you. If it is a struggle and something that you don't feel completely comfortable with, this is not the career for you.

Freelance writers must also be detail oriented, because their job is a journalistic one. The people who read your work are depending on you to give them all the information they need to understand the disease, political issue, or breed you are describing. You must have the kind of mind that will sense what details are important to each subject you are writing about.

Self-discipline is another very important characteristic for a freelance writer. There will be times when you don't feel like writing, when you'd rather be outside playing with your dog. You can't give into these moods; if you do, you won't have a career for very long.

Successful freelance writers are also deadline oriented and can handle the stresses of having one deadline after another on their work calendar. They are also the type of people who understand the importance of deadlines. Nothing is more aggravating to an editor than a writer who blatantly ignores her deadlines.

To enjoy being a freelance writer, you must be able to work alone. Writers spend long hours in the office with no one but a pet or two for company. If you are the type of person that needs constant contact with other humans when you are working, you will be miserable in this career.

Finally, tenacity is a requirement if you plan to be a professional writer. You will need this virtue not only when you are researching your stories but also while trying to make it in this competitive and sometimes difficult profession.

ADVANTAGES

If you love writing and you are crazy about dogs, being a professional dog writer will probably be a dream come true for you. Because writing requires that you immerse yourself in whatever subject matter you are working with, writing about dogs for someone who can't get enough of these wonderful creatures can be a lot of fun.

Freelance writers have a lot of flexibility, both in their schedules and in what they write. Once you are successful, you can pick and choose what you write and when you write it—in terms of time of day, that is. If you are more creative at night, you can work from eight to midnight. If mornings are your thing, six to noon might be your time slot. Or, you can take Fridays off altogether, opting to work on Sunday instead. It's completely up to you.

Name recognition is one of the benefits that comes with successful freelance writing. People start to see your name over and over again in print, and you become a celebrity of sorts. This is especially true once you author a book or two.

Finally, start-up costs are relatively low for freelance writers. All you need is a desk, a chair, a telephone and answering machine, and a personal computer. Along with some talent and business savvy, you are in business.

DISADVANTAGES

Freelance writing is a very difficult field to break into, and it can take many years to forge a successful career. There is a lot of competition out there, and editors can pick and choose among a huge number of seasoned professionals whenever they have work that needs to be done. For this reason, you will probably have to work at another job while you pursue your freelance dream on a part-time basis.

The life of a freelance writer can be a lonely one. Writers spend hours in front of their computers in complete isolation, totally absorbed in the subject at hand. Not everyone is suited to this type of solitary work.

The income earned by freelance dog writers is not usually very high. Even the most successful writers earn only a comfortable living. If you want to get rich writing books and articles, dogs are probably not the best subject for you.

EDUCATION

It is rare to find a successful writer who has not had a formal education. Four-year degrees with majors in journalism, English, or communication arts are the most common. Here you will receive the technical training you need to write accurately and concisely, as well as the worldly knowledge so necessary to being a well-rounded writer.

While you are attending school, try to get as much practical writing experience as you can. Volunteer to write for your school newspaper or a local canine publication. Join a writer's club where you can submit your work to fellow writers and receive criticism on your work. Even though you are planning to write nonfiction in your career, consider taking creative writing courses at your school as well. Developing all your skills as a writer is crucial if you are to find later success in this field.

Learn as much as you can about dogs while you are studying to be a writer. Do volunteer work at your local shelter, and go to dog shows and other canine events. The more you know about your subject matter, the better off you will be.

GETTING A JOB

Your first move once you are ready to begin your freelance writing career is to get yourself published. The easiest way to do this is to write pro bono for a canine publication. Breed club newsletters often accept article submissions, and these are excellent places to get your first byline. Contact the editor and ask her what kinds of articles the publication is looking for. Once you know what they need, go out and write it. With a few of these assignments under your belt, you'll have the beginnings of a dog writing portfolio.

Once you have some published samples of your writing, start researching the various dog magazines that are being published. This includes everything from regional publications to national magazines. Get to know the editorial content of each publication, and develop a feel for their style and audience. Send away for writer's guidelines, and then propose some articles to a number of publications. Be sure to include copies of your published work and detailed information on your educational, writing, and canine background.

It may take a few years, but hopefully an editor somewhere will give you your first big break. Once you've been published in a major canine publication, your chances of getting another article published are significantly increased. At this point, you can begin querying book publishers as well if this is an area you'd like to get into.

Some freelance dog writers start out as editors first, working on a dog publication or for a canine book publisher. Here they learn firsthand what editors are looking for, all the while making valuable contacts for their future career as a freelancer.

SALARY

Newcomers to the freelance dog writing community often have to start out by giving their work away, leaving them with a zero income for at least the first year. Those who are fortunate enough to start to sell their work right away will still need some time before they are getting enough assignments to work full time.

Successful freelance dog writers make anywhere from $20,000

to $75,000 a year, depending on their experience, years in the busi-
ness, and name recognition. There are only a precious few writers
in the upper echelon of the salary range. Most hover somewhere in
the lower numbers.

APPENDIX

PROFESSIONAL ORGANIZATIONS, SCHOOLS, AND

OTHER CAREER-RELEVANT DOG ORGANIZATIONS

PROFESSIONAL ORGANIZATIONS

American Boarding Kennels Association
4575 Galley Road, #400A
Colorado Springs, CO 80915
(719) 591-1113

American Grooming Shop Association
4575 Galley Road, #400A
Colorado Springs, CO 80915
(719) 570-7788

American Pet Boarding Association
P.O. Box 931
Wheeling, IL 60090
(312) 634-9447

American Professional Pet Distributors, Inc. (APPDI)
440 Pinburr Lane
Stone Mountain, GA 30087
(404) 498-5984

American Veterinary Medical Association
930 N. Meacham Road
Schaumburg, IL 60196
(800) 248-2862

Association of Pet Dog Trainers
P.O. Box 385
Davis, CA 95617
(800) PET-DOGS

Association of Small Animal Practitioners
178 Peachtree Street, #299
Atlanta, GA 30303
(800) PRO-0748

Canadian Veterinary Medical Association
339 Booth Street
Ottawa, Ontario
Canada K1R 7K1
(613) 236-1162

Dog Writer's Association of America
Pat Santi, Secretary
173 Union Road
Coatesville, PA 19320
(610) 384-2436

International Association of Home Pet Care Services
38 Sunset Drive
Kensington, CA 94707
(415) 524-0451

International Association of Pet Cemeteries
P.O. Box 1346
South Bend, IN 46624
(219) 277-1115

National Animal Control Association
P.O. Box 480851
Kansas City, MO 64148
(913) 768-0607

National Association of Dog Obedience Instructors (NADOI)
Attn: Corresponding Secretary
729 Grapevine Highway, Suite 369
Hurst, TX   76054-2085
[no phone # available]

National Association of Professional Pet Sitting
1200 G Street N.W., Suite 760
Washington, DC 20005
(202) 393-3317

National Dog Groomers Association
P.O. Box 101
Clark, PA 16113
(724) 962-2711

North American Veterinary Technician Association
P.O. Box 224
Battle Ground, IN 47920
(317) 742-2216

Northwest Professional Groomers Association
10220 29th Street E. #5
Puyallup, WA 98372
(206) 841-2544

Pet Industry Distributors Association (PIDA)
5024-R Campbell Road
Baltimore, MD 21236
(301) 256-8100

Pet Sitters International
418 E. King Street
King, NC 27021-9163
(800) 380-PETS

Professional Association of Pet Industries
4311 Treat Boulevard
Concord, CA 94521
(415) 674-0500

Professional Dog Groomers Association/Canada
Diane Sparham
182 Province Street
Hamilton, Ontario
Canada L8H 4H8
(416) 549-4135

Professional Handlers Association
15810 Mt. Everest Lane
Silver Spring, MD 20906
(301) 924-0089

Western Humane Educators Association
Micki Zeldes
Marin Humane Society
171 Bel Marin Keys Boulevard
Novato, CA 94947
(415) 883-4621

EDUCATIONAL ORGANIZATION

Association of Veterinary Medical Colleges
1023 15th Street, N.W., 3rd Floor
Washington, DC 20005
(202) 371-9195

VETERINARY SCHOOLS

Auburn University
College of Veterinary Medicine
104 Green Hall
Auburn, AL 36849-5517
(334) 844-4546; fax: (334) 844-3697
Web site: http://www.vetmed.auburn.edu

University of California/Davis
School of Veterinary Medicine
Davis, CA 95616
(916) 752-1360; fax: (916) 752-2801
Web site: http://www.vetnet.ucdavis.edu

Colorado State University
College of Veterinary Medicine
Fort Collins, CO 80523
(303) 491-7051; fax: (303) 491-2250
Web site: http://www.vetmed.colostate.edu/index.html

Cornell University
College of Veterinary Medicine
317 Veterinary Research Tower
Ithaca, NY 14853-6401
(607) 253-3771; fax: (607) 253-3701
Web site: http://www.zoo.vet.cornell.edu

University of Florida
College of Veterinary Medicine
215 S.W. 16th Avenue, P.O. Box 100125
Gainesville, FL 32610-0125
(904) 392-2381; fax: (904) 392-8351
Web site: http://www.vetmed.ufl.edu

University of Georgia
College of Veterinary Medicine
Athens, GA 30602
(706) 542-3461; fax: (706) 542-8254

University of Illinois/Urbana
College of Veterinary Medicine
2001 South Lincoln Avenue
Urbana, IL 61801
(217) 333-2760; fax: (217) 333-4628
Web site: http://www.cvm.uiuc.edu

Iowa State University
College of Veterinary Medicine
2508 Veterinary Administration
Ames, IA 50011-1250
(515) 294-1250; fax: (515) 294-8341
Web site: http://www.vetmed.iastate.edu

Kansas State University
College of Veterinary Medicine
Trotter Hall 101E
Manhattan, KS 66506
(913) 532-5660; fax: (913) 532-5884
Web site: http://www.vet.ksu.edu

Louisiana State University
School of Veterinary Medicine
Baton Rouge, LA 70803
(504) 346-3200; fax: (504) 346-5702
Web site: http://www.vtsas.vetmed.lsu.edu

Michigan State University
College of Veterinary Medicine
G-100 Veterinary Medical Center
East Lansing, MI 48824-1314
(517) 355-6509; fax: (517) 336-1037
Web site: http://www.cvm.msu.edu

University of Minnesota
College of Veterinary Medicine
455 Veterinary Teaching Hospital
1365 Gortner Avenue
Street Paul, MN 55108
(612) 624-6244; fax: (612) 624-8753

Mississippi State University
College of Veterinary Medicine
Drawer V
Mississippi State, MS 39762
(601) 325-1131; fax: (601) 325-1498
Web site: http://pegasus.cvm.msstate.edu

University of Missouri
College of Veterinary Medicine
Columbia, MO 65211
(314) 882-7011; fax: (314) 882-2950
Web site: http://www.hsc.missouri.edu/vetmed/docs/umc-cvm.html

North Carolina State University
College of Veterinary Medicine
4700 Hillsborough Street
Raleigh, NC 27606
(919) 829-4210; fax: (919) 821-4452
Web site: http://www2.ncsu.edu/ncsu/cvm/cvmhome.html

Ohio State University
College of Veterinary Medicine
101 Sisson Hall, 1900 Coffey Road
Columbus, OH 43210
(614) 292-1171; fax: (614) 292-7185
Web site: http://www.vet.ohio-state.edu

Oklahoma State University
College of Veterinary Medicine
205 Veterinary Medicine
Stillwater, OK 74078
(405) 744-6648; fax: (405) 744-6633
Web site: http://www.cvm.okstate.edu

Oregon State University
College of Veterinary Medicine
200 Magruder Hall
Corvallis, OR 97331-4801
(503) 737-2098; fax: (503) 737-0502

University of Pennsylvania
School of Veterinary Medicine
110 Rosenthal, 3800 Spruce Street
Philadelphia, PA 19104-6044
(215) 898-8841; fax: (215) 573-8837
Web site: http://www.vet.upenn.edu

Purdue University
School of Veterinary Medicine
1240 Lynn Hall
West Lafayette, IN 47907-1240
(317) 494-7608; fax: (317) 496-1261
Web site: http://www.vet.purdue.edu

University of Tennessee
College of Veterinary Medicine
P.O. Box 1071
Knoxville, TN 37901
(615) 974-7262; fax: (615) 974-4773
Web site: http://www.funnelweb.utcc.utk.edu/vet

Texas A&M University
College of Veterinary Medicine
College Station, TX 77843-4461
(409) 845-5038; fax: (409) 845-5088
Web site: http://www.cvm.tamu.edu

Tufts University
School of Veterinary Medicine
200 Westboro Road
North Grafton, MA 01536
(508) 839-5302, ext. 4700; fax: (508) 839-2953

Tuskegee University
School of Veterinary Medicine
Tuskegee, AL 36088
(334) 727-8174; fax: (334) 727-8177

Virginia-Maryland Regional College of Veterinary Medicine
Virginia Tech Campus
Duckpond Drive
Blacksburg, VA 24061
(540) 231-5821; fax: (540) 231-7367
Web site: http://www.vetmed.vt.edu

Washington State University
College of Veterinary Medicine
Pullman, WA 99164-7010
(509) 335-9515; fax: (509) 335-6094

University of Wisconsin-Madison
School of Veterinary Medicine
2015 Linden Drive W.
Madison, WI 53706
(608) 263-6716; fax: (608) 265-6748

DOG TRAINING SCHOOLS

Affection Dog Training School
330 Capella Avenue
La Habra, CA 90631
(310) 697-0234

Florida Academy of Dog Training
1920 62nd Avenue North
Street Petersburg, FL 33702
(813) 526-3401

Guide Dogs for the Blind
Training Department
P.O. Box 151200
San Rafael, CA 94915-1200
(415) 499-4000

Jo-Thors Dog Academy
3000 Johnson Ferry Place, Suite 209
Marietta, GA 30062
(770) 642-4191

National K-9 School of Dog Training
221 Morrison Road
Columbus, OH 43212
(614) 864-0213

West Virginia Canine College
P.O. Box 2078
Buckhannon, WV 26201
(800) 433-1714

DOG GROOMING SCHOOLS

Academy of Dog Grooming Arts
1900 S. Arlington Heights Road,
Arlington Heights, IL 60005
(847) 228-5700

California School of Dog Grooming
727 W. San Marcos, Suite 105
San Marcos, CA 92069
(800) 949-3746

Michigan School of Canine Cosmetology
3022 S. Cedar Street
Lansing, MI 48910
(517) 393-6311

Michigan School of Dog Grooming
8025 13th Street
Silver Spring, MD 20910
(800) 543-3228

Nash Academy
857 Lane Allen Road
Lexington, KY 40504
(606) 276-5301

New York School of Dog Grooming
248 E. 34th Street,
New York, NY 10016
(800) 541-5541

Pedigree Career Institute
Harbor Maill, Route 1A
The Lynnway
Lynn, MA 01901
(800) 615-3647

Pennsylvania Academy of Pet Grooming
2860 Route 422 West
Indiana, PA 15717
(412) 463-6101

Southern Institute of Pet Grooming
P.O. 313
Central, SC 29630
(864) 639-6872

Tara Lara Academy of K-9 Hair Design
16037 S.E. McLoughlin Boulevard
Portland, OR 97267
(503) 653-7134

Texas All-Breed Grooming School Inc.
1002 Enterprise Place, Suite 100
Arlington, TX 76017
(817) 472-7054

Texas Institute of Pet Design
8617 N. New Braunfels
San Antonio, TX 78217
(210) 822-9355

Wisconsin School of Professional Pet Grooming
N51 W34917 Wisconsin Avenue
P.O. Box 175
Okauchee, WI 53069
(414) 569-9492

VETERINARY ASSISTANCE SCHOOLS

International Correspondence School of Animal Science
925 Oak Street
Scranton, PA 18515
(800) 595-5505, ext. 1895

Professional Career Development Center
3597 Parkway Lane, Suite 100
Norcross, GA 30092
(770) 729-8400

MAJOR DOG PUBLICATIONS

AKC Gazette
American Kennel Club
51 Madison Avenue
New York, NY 10010

Dog Fancy
Fancy Publications
P.O. Box 6050
Mission Viejo, CA 92690

Dogs in Canada
Canadian Kennel Club
89 Skyway Avenue, Suite 200
Etobicoke, Ontario M9Q 6R4
Canada

Dogs in Canada Annual
Canadian Kennel Club
89 Skyway Avenue, Suite 200
Etobicoke, Ontario M9Q 6R4
Canada

Dogs U.S.A.
Fancy Publications
P.O. Box 6050
Mission Viejo, CA 92690

Dog World
P.O. Box 6500
Chicago, IL 60680

INDEX

Advantages of careers
     with dogs, 13–14
animal:
     control officer, 67
     welfare advocate,
          61–62
attorney, 101–102
boarding kennel
     operator, 47–48
commercial:
     artist, 108
     photographer, 113–114
dog trainer, 72–73
editor, 97
freelance writer, 118
groomer, 82
kennel aide, 51–52
marketing specialist, 93
obedience instructor, 77
petsitter, 55–56
professional handler, 87
veterinarian, 32
veterinary:
     assistant, 42–43
     technician, 38–39
Advertisements, 22–23
Agencies, employment, 23
Allergies, 11
Animal:
     control officer, 65–69
     welfare advocate, 60–64
Animals, love of, 10
Artist, commercial,
     106–111
Assistant, veterinary,
     41–44
Attorney, 100–104

Boarding kennel operator,
     46–50

Characteristics, required,
     8–14
Cold calling, 23
Commercial:
     artist, 106–111
     photographer, 111–115
Corporate professions,
     91–104

Cover letters, 25
Creative positions,
     105–121

Disadvantages of careers
     with dogs, 11–13
animal:
     control officer, 67–68
     welfare advocate,
          62–63
attorney, 102
boarding kennel
     operator, 48
commercial artist,
     108–109
dog trainer, 73–74
editor, 97–98
freelance writer, 118–119
groomer, 82–83
kennel aide, 52
marketing specialist, 94
obedience instructor,
     77–78
petsitter, 56–57
professional handler, 88
veterinarian, 32–33
veterinary:
     assistant, 43
     technician, 39
Dog:
     grooming schools,
          132–134
     trainer, 71–75
     training schools,
          131–132
Domestication, 1–2
Duties:
     animal:
          control officer, 65–66
          welfare advocate,
               60–61
     attorney, 109
     boarding kennel
          operator, 46
     commercial:
          artist, 106–107
          photographer, 111–112
     dog trainer, 71
     editor, 96

freelance writer, 116–117
groomer, 80–81
kennel aide, 50–51
marketing specialist, 92
obedience instructor, 76
petsitter, 54
professional handler,
     85–86
veterinarian, 29–31
veterinary:
     assistant, 41
     technician, 36–37

Editor, 95–100
Educational organizations,
     125
Educational requirements:
animal:
     control officer, 68
     welfare advocate, 63
attorney, 102–103
boarding kennel
     operator, 48–49
commercial:
     artist, 109
     photographer, 114
dog trainer, 74–75
editor, 98–99
freelance writer, 119
groomer, 83–84
kennel aide, 52
marketing specialist, 94
obedience instructor,
     78–79
petsitter, 57
professional handler,
     88–89
veterinarian, 33–35
veterinary:
     assistant, 43
     technician, 39–40
Empathy, 9
Employment search:
     advertisements, 22–23
     cold calling, 23
     cover letters, 25
     employment agencies,
          23
     experience, getting, 18–19

internships, 19
interview, 26–27
networking, 20–21, 23
prejob experience, 18–19
resumé, 24–25
school placement, 22
thank-you notes, 27
volunteering, 18, 21
work, part-time, 19
Experience, getting, 18–19

Financial considerations,
    11–12
Freelance writer, 116–121

General dog care
    professions, 45–58
Groomer, 80–85
Grooming schools,
    132–134

Handler, professional,
    85–90
Hands-on work, 70–90
Health:
    care professions, 28–44
    considerations, 10–11
History, 1–7
    breeding, 3
    pet, 4
    work, 3–4
Humane work, 59–69

Income, 11–12
Instructor, obedience,
    75–80
Internet, use of, 16–17
Internships, 19
Interview, 26–27

Job, finding:
    advertisements, 22–23
    cold calling, 23
    cover letters, 25
    employment agencies,
        23
    experience, getting,
        18–19
    internships, 19
    interview, 26–27
    networking, 20–21, 23
    prejob experience, 18–19
    resumé, 24–25
    school placement, 22
    thank-you notes, 27
    volunteering, 18, 21
    work, part-time, 19

Job selection, 15–17

Kennel:
    aide, 50–53
    operator, 46–50
Knowledge, development
    of, 14

Love of animals, 10

Marketing, 15–27
    specialist, 92–95

Networking, 20–21, 23

Obedience instructor,
    75–80

Patience, 9
People skills, 9–10
Personal assessment,
    16–17
Pet:
    industry, 6–7
    sitter, 53–58
Photographer, commercial,
    111–115
Prejob experience, 18–19
Professional:
    handler, 85–90
    organizations, 122–125
Publications, 134

Resumé, 24–25

Salary:
    animal:
        control officer, 69
        welfare advocate, 64
    attorney, 104
    boarding kennel
        operator, 50
    commercial:
        artist, 111
        photographer, 115
    dog trainer, 75
    editor, 100
    freelance writer, 120–121
    groomer, 85
    kennel aide, 53
    marketing specialist, 95
    obedience instructor,
        79–80
    petsitter, 58
    professional handler,
        89–90
    veterinarian, 36

veterinary:
    assistant, 44
    technician, 41
School placement, 22
Schools:
    dog training, 131–132
    grooming, 132–134
    veterinary, 126–131
    assistance, 134
Self exploration, 16–17
Social rewards, 13
Strength, 10–11

Technician, veterinary,
    36–41
Thank-you notes, 27
Trainer:
    dog, 71–75
    obedience, 75–80
Traits, required, 8–14

Veterinarian, 29–36
Veterinary:
    assistance schools, 134
    assistant, 41–44
    schools, 126–131
    technician, 36–41
Volunteering, 18, 21

Welfare, animal, advocate,
    60–64
Work, part-time, 19
World Wide Web, 16–17
Writer, freelance, 116–121